101 MISTAKES ALL

GOLFERS MAKE

(AND HOW TO FIX THEM)

JON SHERMAN

Practical Golf, Inc.
www.practical-golf.com

101 Mistakes All Golfers Make (and how to fix them)/ Jon Sherman. —1st ed.
ISBN-13: 978-0692605226 (Practical Golf, Inc.)
ISBN-10: 0692605223

This book is dedicated to a few people.

To my wife – I never knew how happy I could be until I met you.

To my son – I hope one day we can stroll down the fairways together.

To my parents – Thank you for your unconditional love, sacrifices, and support.

To my brother – For teaching me how to think differently.

To all my friends – You have made my life fun and complete.

"Success depends almost entirely on how effectively you learn to manage the game's two ultimate adversaries: the course and yourself."

JACK NICKLAUS

Preface

First off, I want to thank you for purchasing this book.

I've spent more than 20 years studying, practicing, and playing this game. I have a deep love for golf that goes down to my core just like you. The reason I wanted to write this book is to share everything I have learned over the years.

The twist is that it is coming from a player's perspective.

There are so many great golf books out there, but teachers are usually the ones writing them. While the information they offer is legitimate, I sometimes believe that it gets lost in translation because it can either be overly technical, or the concepts discussed are not communicated in a simple enough way.

So why listen to me? Well I have been through it all. I have conquered every single scoring milestone in various stages of my golfing life. I have broken 100, 90, 80, and even 70. I have competed in U.S. Open qualifiers, college tournaments, and various other amateur events. I currently play between a 0-2 handicap, so I know what it takes to get to the highest level of golf.

More importantly, I have been out there on the course thousands of times with players like you.

Along the way I have made more mistakes than I would like to admit, and witnessed even more from other golfers. I learned from every single one of them.

Curtis Strange once said that golf is a difficult game, but it doesn't have to be a complicated one. That is what this book is about.

I am going to take you through 101 mistakes that all golfers make, and what you can do to fix them. You will learn how to improve your mental game, course strategy, swing technique, practice methods, and much more. Nothing in this book is complicated, and a golfer at any level can improve using just a few of these suggestions.

Keep in mind that 101 is a big number, and you should not try to conquer all of these mistakes at once. I want this book to be your reference guide for years to come. If you focus on achieving just 3-4 of these at a time, I can guarantee you will become a better golfer, and more importantly enjoy the game more.

Jon Sherman
Owner, Practical Golf

[1]

Copying Someone Else's Swing

Golf swings are like fingerprints; they are unique to us all. The lists of characteristics that make up a good golf swing are endless, and there have been many long books written about them. Despite what some teachers would try to convince you of, there is not one right way to do it.

We all have different physical abilities and body types. Some players are not capable of making certain moves because they lack proper coordination and flexibility. That doesn't mean they can't hit a golf ball properly, they just need to work on a swing that takes into account their particular set of abilities.

This is the exact reason you should never try to copy someone else's swing, especially a professional golfer's. The best way to give yourself a chance at having a great swing is to work with what you've got, rather than making enormous changes that don't fit your capabilities.

You will waste a ton of time trying to fit a square peg into a round hole by trying to copy a swing that doesn't suit you.

[2]

Expecting Too Much From Your Round

You've only played golf three times during the last few months, and you decide to get out there with some friends on the weekend. On the third hole you hit a terrible shot, and all of a sudden you're completely distraught and the rest of your round is a disaster because you continue to get angry with yourself for every bad shot you hit.

Why? What else were you expecting?

The greatest thing preventing all of us from enjoying golf more are our unrealistic expectations. Golf is mostly a game of mistakes, and if you don't play all that much then you're probably going to be making a ton of them out on the course!

As much as we would like, we can't have it both ways. If you don't have time to practice, or even play that much, then you should expect to be hitting mostly bad shots on the course.

Is that fun? Well it can be if you try and enjoy your time getting fresh air, and enjoying the walk with your buddies. If you're completely focused on the bad shots you were hitting, then it might not be worth the $75 you spent for the torture session. What's amazing about golf is that all it takes is a few great shots to make it worth it.

Those are the swings that keep us coming back for more.

Golf is a difficult game, but it doesn't necessarily have to interfere with whether or not you have fun. The easiest way to help fix that problem is to be realistic with your expectations.

[3]

Swinging for Divots

One of the biggest myths out there is that you need to take a divot in order to hit a great golf shot. Well, it's actually not true.

Several instructors have done experiments with radar devices like Trackman that prove you can hit the ball effectively without taking a monster divot that you see the pros making on TV. In fact, you don't even need to take a divot at all.

Watch Steve Stricker hit a golf ball. He picks it absolutely clean many times with his irons. He is one of the best golfers in the world, so that should be proof right there that divots are not necessary.

The actual key to hitting a golf ball properly with your irons is to make contact with the ball first, and then your club should interact with the turf afterwards. Many players misinterpret taking divots for hitting better shots, and often swing way too steeply, taking a huge chunk out of the ground before the ball.

So don't think that you have to take an extremely steep swing with your irons in order to hit towering golf shots. The most important thing is to make sure you are making contact with the ball first, rather than the ground.

[4]

Practicing Longer Putts

Golfers tend to have things a bit backwards when it comes to putting. They are more concerned with trying to sink putts that they have very little chance of making. It often leads to the one thing that holds most high-handicappers from shooting lower scores, which is three putting.

Your chances of making putts from outside of 8 feet are very low. They are actually shockingly low. The average golfer makes five-foot putts only 50% of the time. Go out to 10 feet, and that number drops down to 20%. From 20 feet, your chances sink to about 6%.

The only distance from which you have a decent chance of making putts is inside 8 feet, which is why your practice should mostly be focused on these distances. If you can be confident in "knee knocker" territory you can drop some serious strokes.

Most golfers assume the difference between shooting a 102 and a 96 will occur through improving their swing and hitting more quality shots from the tee and fairway. While this may be true, many strokes are lost at this level on the putting green. Almost 40% of your score can occur with the putter in your hand.

However, most players invest almost none of their practice time on putting.

The putts from 4 to 8 feet are so pivotal because they are the ones for par and bogey. If you make them, you will give yourself a positive mental boost that will carry over to the next hole. If you miss them, it often results in that sinking feeling that can ruin your momentum.

Practicing from these distances is often considered boring, but if you can see the ball going in the hole over and over again on the practice green, this positive mental feedback will transfer over to the golf course. Additionally, boosting your confidence on the shorter putts won't make the longer ones seem as daunting on the course, and you will begin to eliminate three putts that result in bogey or double bogey.

This is one of the simplest ways to lower your handicap, and it doesn't involve spending hundreds of dollars on lessons and hours on the driving range. Commit to the knee-knocker putts, and you will shoot lower scores. It's a guarantee!

[5]

Not Enough Club

When you're finished reading this book, this piece of advice is one of the five things you should remember because it's that important.

GAME GOLF has compiled data on millions of shots taken by amateurs at the time this book was written. Do you want to know what was the biggest trend they found?

94% of golfers were missing the majority of their approach shots on the short side of the green.

The cardinal sin of the recreational golfer is that they step up to the ball and choose the wrong club for the shot. This happens for many reasons, but it mostly boils down to two things:

1. They don't have the right yardage information.
2. They believe they hit the ball farther than they actually do.

Instead of choosing a club based on your best swing, choose one that represents your average strike. For example, if you have 145 yards to the middle of the green, and you know that the maximum distance you can hit your 7-iron is around that number, the 6-iron might be the smarter play. The likelihood is that you won't hit the ball perfectly, but you can still get it on the green with a less-than-perfect swing.

Being honest with yourself on how far you hit each club will allow you to hit more greens, which will result in more birdies and pars rather than bogeys and double bogeys.

It's that simple.

[6]

Impatience

All golfers want to break through to the next level of scoring. However, most don't understand just how difficult it is.

If you are someone who is shooting in the mid 90s, and you are hoping to one day get down to the mid to low 80s, it's best to understand that the journey is not going to be a straight line. You're not all of a sudden going to start shooting an 83 when most of your rounds aren't even close to that number.

Sometimes we get a little impatient, and expect it to happen quickly.

An important concept to understand is that most golfers will end up shooting the scores they are comfortable with. If you are currently averaging a 95, you might find that rounds where you are on pace to do much better usually end in some kind of major blowup. You could be only 3-4 holes away from posting an 87, but because you don't have much experience breaking 90 you become extremely nervous, and end up making a few mistakes that result in you shooting your normal round.

Do not get discouraged when that happens! Breaking through to the next level is just as psychological as it is physical. There's no question you have to put the work in to get there, and try to play more, but you also have to experience those failures before you can break through.

The next time you are having a magical round and you crash and burn at the end, don't lose hope. Try to learn from the experience rather than being discouraged by it. One day you are going to break through and shoot that 87, and then you will know you can do it.

Success in golf is usually built in minor steps rather than drastic jumps in scoring. Try to be patient with yourself along the way, and you will eventually get to where you want to be if you remain persistent.

[7]

Swinging Harder Into the Wind

When the wind is blowing in your face, your first instinct is to swing harder. This is the complete opposite of what you should be doing!

Spin is your worst enemy when things are getting gusty on the golf course.

When you try and swing harder, you'll naturally put more spin on the ball, and if you don't strike it perfectly that will cause sidespin. As a result your slices will go much farther right, and your hooks will be heading more left than normal.

Even if you hit the ball straight, it will balloon straight up into the air, and go well short of your intended distance when it has too much spin.

Solid strikes are rewarded when the wind is in your face, and that should be your main focus. Trying to fight the wind by swinging harder is just going to result in even bigger mistakes.

The rule of thumb is to take more club than you think you need, and try to make a more controlled, compact swing. Playing the ball a little back in your stance will help you keep the ball a little lower, which is also one of the keys to playing in the wind.

Don't get into a fight with Mother Nature; you will lose almost every time. Try to keep the ball lower with a longer club selection, and focus on keeping your swings as smooth as possible.

[8]

Not Investing Time in Your Short Game

Golfers can become obsessed with working on their swings, and it might not be the best use of their time.

Your overall goal when you are working on your game is to lower your scores; that should be obvious to almost everyone. However, many of us don't have unlimited time to do this. Practice time is usually squeezed in between work, family obligations, and all of the other things in life that get in the way of golf.

If your goal is to get better, and you are short on time, you need to plan your practice sessions effectively.

Grooving your swing does not happen quickly. You generally have to take lessons and spend hours changing your habits. On top of that, you then have to bring it out on the course.

This is exactly why making swing changes are very difficult, even at the pro level. It is certainly a worthy pursuit for any golfer, but you must be realistic about the inherent challenges you will face.

Let's say you are operating at about 75% swing efficiency, meaning your swing is not the best it could be, but it's not completely far off from being great. To go from 75% to 90% might take a ton of time and effort.

There might be another part of your game that is operating at a much lower efficiency, and you can make huge strides very quickly if you focus your efforts there. On top of that, it can lower your scores dramatically.

I am of course speaking about your short game, and what is occurring 100 yards and in. If golfers spent half the time worrying about their short games than they do about their full swings, scores would be dropping like a stone around the world. It is the best bang for your buck in terms of time invested and saving strokes on the course.

Challenge yourself to work on your putting, chipping, and pitch shots exclusively for a few practice sessions.

One of the hardest truths about golf is that all golfers will not have the ability to master their full swing, but every player has the ability to have a great short game. If you can hang your hat on your wedges and putter, you can break through to the next level of golf that you have been wanting. You just have to make it a priority.

[9]

Playing Golf in a Cart

Walking the golf course has become a lost art. Most facilities encourage players to take a cart now because it increases their revenue, and can speed up play. Players are more than happy to oblige because walking the golf course can be physically taxing.

This is an absolute shame.

You are missing out on two huge benefits if you never walk a course.

The first is exercise. Did you know that walking a typical golf course will net you about 5-7 miles, and can burn as many as 1000 calories? It's actually one of the best workouts you can do without even realizing you are exercising! Most of us have a hard time committing to a fitness routine and finding the time to do it. Walking the golf course can help fix both of those issues (not to mention save you a few bucks in cart fees).

The second reason you should ditch the cart is because you will likely play better.

Have you ever hit a bad shot and then sped on the cart to your ball? You probably took no time to calm yourself down, or even think about what your strategy should be. Our minds naturally speed up when we make a mistake, and driving on the cart can make things go even faster.

The time it takes to walk between shots is a great way to clear your mind. Take a look at the trees, and enjoy your time outside. You should also be focusing on your next shot and thinking about your options. If you are in a cart this will be harder to do. When the game speeds up it often leads to unforced mental errors because you did not completely think things through.

So if you're able to, think about walking the course. It might lower your scores, and get you in better shape.

[10]

Wasting Money on Golf Balls

Despite what golf ball companies tell you, it is not necessary for you to spend $50 on a dozen golf balls. In fact, it actually might be harming your game if you are playing a pro-level ball when it's not necessary.

There are plenty of balls in the $20-$30 range that can suit most golfers. Technology has come a long way, and many of the less expensive balls offer plenty of durability, distance, and spin around the greens.

Golf is an expensive game, and this is one way you can guarantee yourself some savings. Don't think your game is going to suffer if you play the less-expensive ball. It most certainly will not!

[11]

Not Playing Enough Break

You may have heard the term "miss your putt on the pro side." That phrase refers to one of the best pieces of putting advice out there, which is to give yourself more room on the higher side of the hole for putts that are breaking in one direction.

Most golfers do not play enough break, and end up missing on the lower side of the cup. If a putt is clearly breaking left to right, you will give yourself a better opportunity to make it if you aim further than you think on the left side.

The reason why this is a good piece of advice is that most amateurs do not hit their putts with enough speed. If their aim was not high enough, then the ball is already past the low side of the cup when it looses its momentum.

The next time you are on the practice green, try to find a putt that breaks in one direction. See if you can keep all of your misses on the high side. This will help you start to understand why this concept is so important.

[12]

Forgetting 18 Holes Is a Long Time

How many times have you reached the back nine and realized what was happening on the second hole was not only a distant memory, but something that could have been avoided?

There is plenty of time to recover from mistakes that occur earlier in your round. 18 holes of golf is like an epic blockbuster movie. There is going to be triumph, heartbreak, and even filler scenes where not much is happening. This is the exact reason we all get hooked on golf. Each round is its own unique story where so many things can happen.

When things don't go your way for a few holes, you can still be the comeback kid who pulls off the improbable win when the odds are stacked against you. There's always a moment where you can turn things around, and there is usually plenty of time left in your round to do it.

One way to assure that it won't happen is to give up hope.

A common trait amongst most great golfers is an ability to maintain their perspective during a round. They try to keep their focus on the shot at hand.

So keep fighting and remain positive. Good things can happen, and maybe you will have an amazing story to tell your buddies on the 19th hole about how you turned things around after a dreadful start.

[13]

Deceleration in Your Short Game

The most common mistake of the average golfer in their short game is deceleration at impact on chips and pitches. It leads to chunks, shanks, and skulls. All of these are ugly words, and we certainly want no part of them on the golf course.

This is one of the main things holding back most golfers from breaking 100 and 90. Wasting precious strokes around the greens results in the dreaded double bogey, which is one of the main reasons you might be struggling to reach these milestones.

Deceleration occurs mostly out of fear of committing to the shot because you are not confident in your technique. What's the quickest way to solve this issue? Well, spending more practice time in this area of the game couldn't hurt.

One of the reasons you are decelerating at impact is because you are not rotating your body. Most golfers are striking their chips and pitches with only their hands and arms, and their upper body is not moving at all.

The way to fix this is to get your hips rotating, and let your body do the work. The club and your arms are just along for the ride.

It's important to keep track of your chest, or belt buckle during these shots. If you are rotating from the hips, they will be pointing behind the ball at the back of your swing, and in front of the ball when you complete your follow through.

If you can focus on rotating through the ball it will help prevent deceleration, and you will begin making more consistent contact on these shots.

[14]

Forgetting Sunscreen

Golf is a great way to spend time outdoors, but unfortunately we expose ourselves to the sun quite a bit during a round. Skin cancer is a major problem for golfers, and you should be protecting yourself every time you are out on the course.

Here are some sobering statistics from the American Academy of Dermatology:

- One in five Americans will develop skin cancer in their lifetime
- Melanoma incidence rates have been increasing for the last 30 years
- Approximately 75 percent of skin cancer deaths are from melanoma

Skin cancer is one of the cancers that have been linked to lifestyle choices. There is no debate that exposing yourself to the sun without protection will increase your chances of developing skin cancer.

So what can you do to protect yourself on the course?

For starters, never play golf without a hat. Your face is the most vulnerable spot on your body, and it needs a physical barrier. There are plenty of products out there that have SPF built into them. For maximum protection, wearing a bucket hat is the best choice since it will cover your ears, neck, and almost your whole face.

Secondly, you should always play with sunscreen on. The rule of thumb is to apply sunscreen about 15-20 minutes before you are going outside so it has time to take effect. More importantly, you should be re-applying every 2 hours.

The sun is strongest between 10am – 2pm, so if possible you should avoid it completely during those hours, but this is sometimes difficult to do as a golfer. You should also be monitoring your skin for any changes, especially if you have moles. Golfers should make it a habit to visit a dermatologist once a year to make sure a professional can spot anything that needs to be tested.

Skin cancer is a very serious disease, and golfers need to take it seriously.

[15]

Pars and Birdies to Break 90 and 100

Many players believe their goal on every hole is to make a par or a birdie. If you're a single-digit handicap, this might be a reasonable expectation. However, if you are looking to shoot in the 90s, or even in the 80s, this is actually the reason why you can't reach these milestones (that might sound confusing).

Breaking 100 and 90 is not primarily about hitting great shots; it is actually more about limiting mistakes. If your target score on a hole is par or birdie, then you are going to force yourself into making aggressive shots, feeling like you are trying to keep up with this score.

Let's go through a hypothetical example of a hole:

John Q golfer tees off on a par 4 and sends his drive well off target into the trees. He's angry with himself, and all he can think about is how he is going to get his ball near the green with his second shot. John is so focused on par, he neglects to realize that in order to get to the green he'll have to pull off a shot that has about .0001% of working out.

Rather than taking his medicine and punching his ball out to safety in an effort to make bogey at worst, John goes for broke and tries to thread his ball through a few sets of trees. Not surprisingly, he hits another tree and goes on to make a triple bogey. The rest of his round is ruined, and he ultimately shoots a 104.

Rather than fall victim to these types of mistakes, trying to play for bogey at worst on every hole will help remove some of the mental pressure. Remember, 18 bogeys is a 90 on most courses. That isn't so bad!

If you can re-adjust your expectations for the kind of score you are trying to shoot, you will actually find it much easier to reach your goals. One of the most important parts of improving as a golfer is managing your expectations, especially with scoring.

[16]

The First Shot Is Your Most Important One

If you were to poll golfers about the shot that scared them the most, it would absolutely be their opening tee shot. Every player gets nervous on the first tee box whether or not they show it, even the pros. Everyone is watching you, the pressure is on, and you don't want to embarrass yourself.

We've all been there.

There are a few ways to get past this, and the first step is to understand that you are not alone! While it may not cure your nerves completely, here is a list of things that can help overcome your first tee jitters:

- If you have time to hit balls before your round, focus your last 5-8 shots visualizing the first tee shot. Practice with the exact same club you will be using, and try to recreate the shot as best as you can mentally.

- The first tee is where your pre-shot routine can pay huge dividends. If you go through a familiar process that takes the same amount of time, you will have less time to think about the pressure you are under.

- Realize that whatever the outcome of the shot, your round will not hang in the balance. Plenty of golfers have gone on to have great rounds after disastrous opening tee shots. Yours is no different.

Stop thinking that this is the most important shot of your round, because it isn't.

[17]

Believing a New Club Will Fix Your Swing

This is a tricky one because it goes against what hundreds of millions of advertising dollars spent by golf club manufacturers have been telling you for years.

Getting a new driver or set of irons is very exciting for any golfer. We all love new toys and the promise of how they can improve our performance. A new club is a clean mental slate, which actually can be priceless for a golfer. We can throw away all of the terrible memories we had with our old driver, and start a new relationship with a club that claims to solve the issue we had previously.

Not to burst your bubble, but this isn't entirely true. Playing the right clubs for your game, and taking advantage of new technology, is certainly a worthwhile investment. You should get fitted with the correct shafts and style of club for your level of play.

Getting your equipment right is an important part of giving yourself the best opportunity to improve. However, don't think the work is done. You are the operator of the golf club, and ultimately it's up to you whether or not you will put a good swing on the ball.

All of the technology in the world won't be able to fix that.

If you are a player that is constantly switching clubs and placing the blame elsewhere...well maybe it's time to start looking at who the captain of the ship is.

Golf clubs can only do so much for your game. At some point we all need to take a hard look at ourselves, and try to put the work in to solve whatever issues might be plaguing us. Spending $400 on a new driver isn't always the solution. You might just be kicking the can down the road.

[18]

Gripping the Club Too Tightly

We all remember that line from the movie **Happy Gilmore**, "I'm just easing the tension baby!"

It's actually one of the best pieces of advice out there.

Tension in the body is one of the main reasons golfers fail to make a proper swing, and it all starts with your hands. When you grip the club too tightly you engage all kinds of muscles in your body that are counterintuitive to making a fluid, controlled swing.

In an effort to hit the ball farther, many golfers will tense up and strangle the grip of the club with their hands. Unfortunately, it results in the exact opposite outcome than they intended.

Try experimenting on the range with different grip pressures, and try to feel the weight of the club in your hand. If you're gripping too tightly, then you may not be able to feel a thing, which is not ideal.

[19]

Living on the Driving Range

The driving range can be an important place to fine tune your game and improve your performance on the course. There is a huge caveat though, and it has to do with how you practice and how often you are spending your time on the golf course under actual pressure.

Many players assume that by showing up to their local practice facility 4-5 times a week and pounding 100-200 balls like a machine, it will automatically lower their scores.

It won't, and there are a couple of reasons why.

The first has to do with how you practice. If you just mindlessly hit balls with the same clubs over and over again, you're not developing any kind of skill that can be applied to a real round of golf. Each time you hit a shot on the course you have a different target and club in your hand. Sometimes you will wait several minutes between swings. There's no opportunity to hit your 7-iron 10 times in a row before it actually counts.

This is exactly why you should try to put some pressure on yourself at the driving range and make a game out of it.

Try playing an imaginary 18 holes where you have to pick a different target and club before each swing. Or pick 5 targets that are all different distances for various kinds of wedge shots. Every shot should have purpose, and require you to think about it before you swing, just like you would (hopefully) be doing on the golf course.

The second reason why investing hours on the range might not pay off is if you are not spending enough time on the actual golf course. A large part of improving as a golfer occurs when you...well, play golf!

There is no substitute for getting on the course and feeling the nerves and tension before you hit a shot. If you're on the range too much, you will never gain the experience necessary to cope with those feelings, and produce the same kind of shots you know you are capable of hitting during a practice session.

If you can try to balance the time you spend practicing with the time you spend on the actual golf course, you will begin to feel more comfortable as a golfer. Simulating a round of golf certainly helps, but there is no substitute for the real thing.

[20]

You Lack Etiquette

This should go without saying, but the last thing you want to do as a golfer is something that distracts your playing partners, or worse, puts another golfer in danger. Etiquette is an important part of the game. Here is a list of 10 friendly reminders:

1. Always be aware when someone is about to swing and please remain quiet. There's nothing worse than listening to your playing partners discuss the shots they just hit while you are trying to hit yours!

2. Be mindful of someone else's line of sight as they prepare for their shot, and remain as still as possible when they are ready to swing. Also keep in mind your shadow can be distracting.

3. Never walk in someone else's line on the putting green.

4. If you hit a wayward shot, please yell "FORE" as loud as you possibly can. This might sound extreme, but you could be saving someone's life.

5. Don't lose your temper and have a cursing tirade. Nobody wants to be around that golfer.

6. If your partners are constantly waiting for you, please speed up.

7. Always repair your ball marks on the green.

8. Turn off your cell phone ringer! Don't spend your round on the phone either; it's rude.

9. It's generally not a good idea to give another golfer unsolicited swing advice during a round.

10. Please rake the bunker when you are done with it. There's nothing worse than having your ball come to rest in someone else's footmarks.

[21]

Driver Is the Only Club You Hit off the Tee

Making smart decisions with his club selection off the tee was one of the main highlights of Jack Nicklaus' career. His number one priority was to keep the ball in play at all costs, and get it on the fairway. It didn't matter to him which club he used to accomplish that goal.

There was a story about the Golden Bear in the book *Golf is Not a Game of Perfect* (which you should read) that summarized his strategy off the tee. Tom Kite was playing with him in the PGA Championship on a grueling 7,200 yard setup, back when players were still using wooden drivers. On the 4th hole Nicklaus hooked a driver, and it was the worst shot that Kite ever saw him hit. That was the last time Jack used his driver the entire round, and it took a lot of discipline to do that.

If that strategy was good enough for the greatest golfer of all time, then it could work out for you too.

It makes total sense why players want to use their drivers all of the time. It is the most expensive club in the bag, it is fun to swing, and it's all you hear about in the golf world. But don't let that fool you into thinking your driver is the only club you should be hitting off the tee!

Golfers these days have an enormous lust for power, and are on a mission to launch the ball as far as humanly possible. There's only one problem. It's not helping them lower their scores in most cases. If you're taking your driver out of the bag 14 times a round, and you can't keep the ball in play most of the time, then maybe it is time to explore Plan B.

Power golf is only effective if you have reasonable accuracy as well. There's no advantage to being 50 yards closer to the green if your ball is stuck in some bushes, out of bounds, or behind a tree. This is why using your 3-wood, hybrids, or long irons off the tee might be the answer for you on certain holes.

Golfers can't escape one simple rule. Your margin of error increases with a longer shaft and a lower club head loft. The tee shot is arguably the most important shot in golf because it sets the tone for your hole. Why not give yourself the best chance at being successful if the hole you're playing has a challenging tee shot?

Golf can be a much easier game when you're closer to the fairway, and one of the ways to do that is to stop assuming you should only be hitting your driver on the tee box.

[2 2]

Standing Over the Ball for Too Long

How many times have you stood over your ball before a shot for too long? You're staring at it and fidgeting around like James Brown on the stage. Twenty seconds have passed, and now you're even more terrified because a few negative thoughts have crept into your mind.

"Don't hit it right, don't hit it right...DON'T HIT IT RIGHT!"

Golfers at all levels do this. It generally doesn't lead to a great shot when you've wasted all of this time and not committed to your shot. You can fix this by coming up with a pre-shot routine. Going through the same process every time will help you commit to the shot, and this will help prevent these jitters before you actually swing.

Committing to your shot is the most important thing you can do to give yourself the best opportunity for it to be successful. Try to work on limiting the amount of time you spend hovering over the ball.

[23]

Forgetting to Enjoy Yourself

So far this book has talked a lot about strategy, practice routines, and the mental side of golf. While these are all important to becoming a better golfer, they are worthless if you are missing one key element on the course. Are you enjoying yourself?

Golf is an extremely time-consuming activity. It can take us away from our family for hours at a time, and only other golfers would understand why we are willing to make such a strong time commitment to the game.

A majority of players are worried about their score first and foremost. When you're done with your round everyone will always ask you what your score was, because it's a way to measure ourselves against one another. While we're all worried about where we stack up against each other, we sometimes forget whether or not we had fun playing.

The funny thing is that if golfers spent more time worrying about enjoyment, then their scores might actually drop.

Your mental state during a round of golf is one of the key determining factors in how well you will play. Have you ever played a round with friends where no one was keeping score? If you haven't, give it a shot one time. You'll be shocked by how many great shots you will hit, and how much fun you will have doing it. The reason why this happens is because you don't have the burden of your score weighing you down.

Our own worries and expectations are the greatest roadblocks to shooting our best scores. While it's not always easy to do, if you can take the attitude that golf is supposed to be fun before anything else, you will probably allow yourself to play better.

[24]

Not Practicing at Home

The driving range is not the only place you can put in meaningful work on your golf game. Depending on the space of your home and your backyard (if you have one), you can work on almost every part of the game.

At the minimum, you can get yourself a putting mat, which can help you hone your stroke. There are a ton of useful putting trainer aids on the market that can help with your alignment and stroke.

If you have space in your backyard then investing in a couple of chipping nets is a must. You might have to be willing to sacrifice a few patches of grass in the process though!

Having a great chipping and pitching game is all about muscle memory. If you can start to feel the distances in your backyard, then when you're on the course your body and mind will be familiar with shots when you step up to them. That is how you build confidence.

Additionally, investing in a practice net to hit full shots is not a bad idea. While you can't see where the ball is going, you certainly can feel the quality of your ball striking. Working on your tempo, and trying to hit the ball as close to the center of the face as possible, can help groove your swing.

As little as 15-30 minutes a day of this kind of work on your golf game is going to yield tremendous results. Part of playing great golf is routine. If you practice only once a week, and pick up a club every 7-10 days, you won't be able to get into any kind of rhythm. Most of us don't have the time to drive to and from the range or the course every day, so the easy solution can be to get creative with golf practice around the house.

Just don't break any windows or put a hole in your walls.

[25]

Ignoring Your Ball Flight

For decades certain golf instructors have claimed that they had the answers for hitting the ball properly. They would teach a certain technique and claim that it was the "right" swing. Over the years that version of the swing would change, and newer teachers would claim whatever existed before their solution did not take into account the latest research.

All of that is starting to get thrown out of the window, and for good reason. Technology has uncovered that what is happening at impact is the most important thing. It doesn't necessarily matter what your swing plane is, where your hands are at the top of your swing, or even how much your head might move.

Where did the ball go? That's the most important thing.

Golfers have been led to believe that if they didn't meet a certain checklist during their swing, then they were doing it wrong. Hours would be spent trying to fix these technical glitches, and it was probably a complete waste of time for many players.

If you are trying to make changes to your swing, pay complete attention to where the ball is going. This is the most important feedback you will ever need. If you can repeat a move you are comfortable with, and it advances the ball towards your target with reasonable consistency, then you have figured out a version of the golf swing that works for you.

Don't let anyone ever tell you otherwise!

[26]

Playing Unrealistic Shots

How many times have you convinced yourself you can carry the ball over a hazard, or fit your ball between a few sets of trees only to see the shot completely fail? Most golfers overestimate their abilities on the course, and it leads to major blowup holes that can torpedo their rounds.

Just because you are capable of hitting a shot does not mean you should try it.

Read that sentence a few times, and let the words burn into your memory. You might have hit a 3-wood 220 yards off of the ground at the driving range a few times. What you conveniently forgot was that it took you about 12 attempts to do it, and there was no real pressure on you.

Most golfers are more aggressive on the course than they realize. They play shots that they believe have a high probability of working out, but in reality it is quite the opposite.

The gap between pulling off shots in practice versus during a round is quite enormous.

When you're on the range, and you've hit the same shot 15-20 times in a row, you begin to develop a rhythm. On the course you can go a few minutes without taking a swing. It's much more difficult to execute difficult shots when you only get one chance, the pressure is on, and you haven't had the benefit of hitting the same shot over and over again.

Having the discipline to be honest with yourself when evaluating whether or not you should attempt to play a difficult shot is one of the key factors that separate the best golfers from the rest of the pack.

We all want to pull off spectacular shots and take the gamble when the moment presents itself. It's more exciting than just playing the safe shot. Our minds have the memories of all of the great swings on the driving range, and we just assume that we can pull it off.

Sadly this mentality is what prevents certain golfers from shooting better scores. If you can begin to be more realistic with the kinds of shots you are capable of hitting on the golf course, and under real pressure, you will start to limit some of the major mistakes that are holding your scores back.

[27]

Misunderstanding Impact Location

Feedback is a golfer's best friend. One of the most vital things a golfer needs to understand is where they are making contact on the clubface. When you start seeing this after each swing, a very interesting process occurs.

The good news is this is relatively easy to do, and inexpensive. The next time you're at the driving range you can do one of the following methods to find out which part of the club face you are making contact with after every swing:

- Purchase a dry-erase pen and mark the ball beforehand. It will leave a small residue on your club wherever contact was made.

- Use impact tape; a large roll will only cost you about $20.

- Get Dr. Scholls Odor X spray. You can spray your clubface, and ball marks will appear for a few shots.

If you hit 10 shots and take notice after every single one of what happened at impact, your body and mind will start to understand which swings were the ones that led to the best contact (which would be closer to the sweet spot). Conversely, you will start to feel what kind of moves you made in your swing that led to the shots where you made contact with the toe or heel of the club.

Try this out the next time you are at the range, and you will be amazed what you can discover.

[28]

Listening Too Much

If you open your ears up there is a lot of noise in the golf world. TV shows, magazine articles, blog posts, online discussion boards, and even your closest friends are all giving advice on their version of what great golf is.

A lot of this information is technical in nature, meaning they have some thoughts on what your hands should be doing, or what position your club should be at the top of your swing.

A golfer can only handle so much of this before they start getting confused and stifled by all of the information. Often in golf, less is more. Taking just one tip and working on it by itself, while putting the blinders on, works best.

This might sound a bit bizarre coming from a book that has "101" in the title, but if you notice there is very little specific information about the swing written thus far. There is a reason for that. It is because you can shoot lower scores without worrying about all of the golf jargon that you hear about.

You don't need lag in your swing, perfect shoulder rotation, or any of the other things you hear about all of the time from the top instructors. Try not to feel like you need to listen to every swing tip out there because you think you might be missing out on something.

Remember, less is more.

[29]

Forgetting Drills

Practice by itself doesn't lead to lower scores. Smart, purposeful practice will though. However, it's difficult for the average golfer to come up with a practice plan for themselves that will give structure to their sessions, and simulate some of the real pressure they will experience on the course.

Additionally, some players find practice boring and often can't bring themselves to stick with it.

That's exactly why drills are so great. They do all of that for you. A great practice drill will often get you hitting different shots in succession, get your competitive juices flowing, and make your practice time more effective.

Golf With a Game Plan by Timo Schlitz is a great book that gives a collection of drills for all parts of your game. Get a copy, and keep it in your golf bag for your practice sessions.

[30]

Aiming at the Pin

Unless the pin is right in the middle of an enormous green, there is no good reason the average golfer should be aiming at the flagstick.

Pros and low-handicap golfers know better than to aim at the pin because they pick and choose their spots based on the risk and reward of each placement. Just because it's the only thing sticking out of the ground does not mean that it should be your target for your approach shot.

Your overall goal on any shot is keeping the ball in a safe spot, and avoiding trouble. Golfers needlessly throw away strokes when they take aim at pins that are situated near hazards, bunkers, and steep drop-offs. If you keep your aim at the largest part of the green regardless of where the pin is, you will hit more greens and shoot lower scores. It's not terribly complicated.

Additionally, the payoff that you think is there by aiming at the pin doesn't really exist. Unless you can successfully land the ball within 10 feet of the pin, you are unlikely to make the putt because your chances outside that distance are so low.

To give you a frame of reference, the best any player could do on the PGA Tour in 2015 was averaging 15 feet from 100-125 yards. It's much harder than you think!

You Are Not Ready

If you aren't playing ready golf, then you are not being considerate to the rest of the golf course. Every weekend millions of golfers pack courses around the world, and often times they are stuck waiting on tees for slow groups to play. It's not fun to go through this, and it's detrimental to the overall health of the game.

If you are playing a recreational round of golf with friends, or even wagering a small amount of money, just remember you are not playing in a professional tournament. What you see on TV is extremely slow golf. Players often take forever to go through their routines with their caddies, making sure they get their yardages exactly right and their putts lined up perfectly.

Millions of dollars are on the line so this makes sense.

Don't take your cues from the pros though; you should be playing ready golf at all times. This means that whoever is ready to hit their shot, even if they are out of turn, can go. If you made the highest score on the previous hole, but are ready to go with your tee shot on the next one...hit the shot. You might be closer to the green on your approach shots but your playing partners are still getting ready to hit theirs. Just let them know you are ready to hit and go ahead.

It should go without saying that you should use some judgment and don't put yourself in harms way, or distract any of your playing partners. Ready golf forgoes some of the traditions of the game in favor of making sure the golf course is moving along.

[32]

Wrong Tee Position With Your Driver

A lot of golfers make the mistake of teeing the ball too low with their driver, and keeping the ball in the middle of their stance. This might be costing them a ton of yards, and we all know every single golfer wants to know how to hit the ball further.

There are a few minor tweaks a golfer can make to improve their driving distance. They first must understand that your drives are the only shot where you are trying to swing up on the ball rather than down.

This refers to a concept called angle of attack. Any time a golfer is trying to hit an iron shot properly, they will have a negative angle of attack, which means the club is approaching the ball on a downward path. In order to maximize your distance potential with your driver, you actually need a positive angle of attack, which means that the club should be on an upward trajectory as it makes contact.

It's not completely necessary, but it will help you unlock more distance without having to swing harder.

There are a number of things you can do to help make sure you are swinging up on the ball with your driver to hit the ball farther, but we won't get into those right now. The easiest way to help with this process is to tee the ball higher, and move it as close to your lead foot as possible. These are two small adjustments that actually can add 10-30 yards to your drives without increasing your swing speed.

Just be aware, results may vary.

[33]

Worrying What Your Playing Partners Think

Everyone gets nervous on the golf course. You may have played with a great golfer before who looked calm and collected throughout the whole round. Rest assured, they were just as nervous over a few shots as you were.

Golf can be a terribly embarrassing game, and we are all going to make big mistakes at some point. There are enough things to worry about during a round. Wondering what your playing partners are thinking should not be one of them.

We are all united by this crazy game, and that means all of us know what it's like to royally screw up a hole. So stop worrying how you look on the course; we are all going through the same fears and nerves.

[34]

No Hybrids in the Bag

If you are a player who struggles to hit their longer irons, and you have not replaced them with hybrids, then you have missed the boat on possibly one of the greatest advancements in equipment technology ever.

The average golfer has always struggled hitting a 3-iron in the air, and it has cost them a ton of strokes. Hybrids make it easy to make proper contact, and more importantly get the ball on a higher trajectory so you have a chance of stopping the ball on, or near the green.

Additionally, hybrids can be an extremely effective weapon off the tee. They will help add distance over your irons, while offering more accuracy than your driver. Think about ditching your 3, 4, or even 5-iron in favor of a hybrid if you are a golfer that has difficulty making proper contact with these clubs. This is one of the easiest ways to improve your game with an equipment change.

[35]

Never Sets Any Goals

If you really want to improve your game, the best way to do it is to set goals for yourself. The best goals are realistic, specific, and measurable. Setting a goal for yourself will help keep you focused and doing the right kind of work to achieve it.

Luckily in golf this is somewhat easy to do since we have our scores and handicap to benchmark ourselves. Let's go through an example of how you can set a goal for yourself that meets all three of these criteria.

"I want to lower my handicap from 18 to 12."

First off, this goal is good because it's within reach. Had you told yourself you wanted to get down to a 4 handicap, you would be setting the bar too high.

If your overall goal is to reach a 12 handicap, now it's time to set specific mini-goals that you will be able to measure your progress against. The best way to do it is to take a hard look at your game, and think about how you are going to accomplish the overall goal.

This particular golfer has noticed that three putting and iron play is the weakness of their game. Here is an example of a subset of goals:

- Practice four times a week for 30 minutes
- Play a minimum of 25 rounds this year
- Average 6/18 greens in regulation per round and 34 putts

It is a very simple list, but writing these down and focusing on these goals throughout the year, will get this golfer to organize him/herself in a way that will allow them to lower their handicap to 12.

Try to make a very simple list for yourself at the beginning of each year, and keep referring back to it to track your progress.

[36]

Driver Over Wedges

Consider the next statement the gospel from the Golfing Gods:

Your driver is not the only key to reaching the next level of scoring.

There is nothing more fun than cranking the ol' big dog at the driving range. Golfers love the long ball; we've been conditioned to think that way because it's all we hear about.

More than half of your shots can occur within 100 yards during a round. This number will likely increase for golfers who are shooting higher-than-average scores. This is where scoring occurs, and your wedges are the key to this puzzle.

Having a stellar short game can save any round of golf. It is a shield that can protect you from almost anything. So stop practicing like you are using your driver 80% of the time on the course!

[37]

Missing Clues on the Green

Part of becoming a more consistent putter is learning to read greens more effectively. Some golfers don't know how to look for some key clues when evaluating the break on their putts. Here are some easy tips that will help you see the break a little more clearly:

- Most greens have a high side and a low side for drainage reasons. Look at the overall slope of the green, and putts will generally break to the lowest point.

- The easiest way to see the line is to read it from the low side of the hole. Think of it like reading a book. It's much easier to see the text with it tilted towards you rather than away from you.

- Use your feet. If you walk around your line do you feel that your toes or heel are higher or lower? That will give you some feedback on which way the green is sloped.

- Know the local topography. Some courses will have a certain point on the course like a creek, or a body of water where putts generally break towards. Try and get the feedback of playing partners who may have had more experience playing that particular course.

- If your first putt travels past the hole keep watching it! This will give you an idea of where the putt will break on your comeback attempt.

[38]

You're a Slicer

One of the most common mistakes golfers make is that they struggle with the slice. No matter what they seem to do, the ball continues to pop up into the sky, and travel to the right of their target.

There are many tips out there that offer remedies to the slice. Most of them are just band-aids because they don't address the real issue of what is going on. If someone tells you to just strengthen your grip and try to close the clubface at impact, your slicing issues will most likely remain.

If the answer were that simple then there would be no slicers.

The real reason you are slicing the ball is not necessarily because you have an open clubface at impact. The path of the club is actually the underlying issue. Slicers have a club path that is coming outside the ball to the inside, or traveling on a leftward path (for a right handed golfer).

Many times golfers will try to fix the issue by aiming further to the left, but this generally makes it worse because the club will come even more across the ball.

One way to solve the slice is actually learning to do the complete opposite. Finding a way to get your club coming from an inside to outside path is really a longer-lasting solution. Most slicers would be terrified to do this, but you actually have to swing the club on a trajectory to the right of the ball.

There is not one way to solve a slice, but ultimately you need to learn to stop the club from coming from the outside of the ball to the inside. Here are a few ways you can experiment with fixing the issue at the driving range:

- Get your shoulders more square to the target, or even a little bit to the right. If you have the ball up in your stance, try moving it back a little bit.
- Think of having a more "round" swing rather than a vertical one. You can exaggerate a more inside swing path to learn what this feels like. Anything you can do to get the club coming from a more inside path is going to help.
- Use a club or an alignment rod as a visual cue. Have it pointing towards the right of your target to give you something to focus on, and help you get the club moving to the outside of the ball after impact.

These are ways you can experiment on your own, but if this is a major issue for you it might be best to schedule a few lessons with a knowledgeable teaching pro.

[39]

Playing With Old Grips

Ben Hogan believed that your grip technique was one of the most important things to get right in your golf game because your hands are the only part of your body that are actually connected to the club.

Grip pressure is an extremely important element in playing great golf. If you are gripping the club too tightly, it will engage muscles in your body that are not helpful to your swing. Feeling relaxed all starts with your hands, and grip pressure plays a large part in that.

If the grips on your clubs are worn down, then you naturally have to grip the club harder to feel like you are holding it securely. This is not good.

Changing your grips once a year is an important equipment tune-up. It's probably one of the most important investments you can make in your game. If you are handy, you can purchase a kit that will allow you to do the work yourself, which can actually save you a decent amount of money.

[40]

Thinking About the Next Hole

Focusing your mind on the task at hand is probably one of the hardest things to do during a round. Our instinct is to start worrying about shots that haven't even occurred yet, and we forget about the most important one, which is the one we're about to hit.

For example, you might have missed the green on an easy par 3, and all of a sudden you're worried about the next hole because you know it is difficult. You may already be condemning yourself to a bogey on the current hole, and thinking about how hard it will be to make par on the next one.

This is understandable, and even the top players in the world fall victim to this kind of thinking from time to time.

Most people assume that the best golfers shoot better scores because they have amazing swings, and are mostly hitting great shots all of the time. While that's certainly an important part of their success, that is not the only reason why they are so good.

Players who have reached the top of the game have an amazing ability to stay present. If they had hit that poor tee shot on the par 3 they would be completely focused on what kind of pitch shot they were about to hit, doing everything in their power to save par.

They will deal with the next hole when they get there.

If you can learn to do this on just a few more shots a round, it will help your game immensely. This is not a part of the game that you will ever completely conquer though. We're only human, and worrying about things that haven't happened yet is just part of natural instincts. But doing it a little bit less is certainly within our reach.

[41]

Your Swing Is All Arms

The golf swing is probably one of the most complicated movements you can make with your body. So many things have to go right to hit the golf ball squarely on the clubface. A common mistake that golfers make is believing that their arms are the focal point of their swings.

In an effort to hit the ball farther, some players forget the most important thing, which is rotation. Their arms dominate their swings, and they don't rotate at all from their hips. If you're doing this, you are missing out on the main elements of a great golf swing.

There are a few ways to check if this is happening to you, and one of the easiest is to focus on where your chest is pointing. Picture an imaginary rod that is connected to your sternum. If you aren't rotating your body when you swing, that rod will barely move away from the ball. Conversely, if your body is rotating properly, this imaginary rod will point at someone who is standing almost completely behind you at the top of your swing.

That will mean you have made a full shoulder turn, which is what you are looking for.

The golf swing is one big unit, and it helps to try to think of everything as being connected. Your arms, hips, and chest should all rotate together as you make your backswing, and hopefully return to the ball completely synchronized.

When your arms dominate your golf swing, it's very difficult to have consistent ball striking.

[42]

Copying the Pros

Watching professional golfers on TV fools us all. They make an extremely difficult game look quite easy. They hit fairways, greens, and then sink almost every putt (or at least the broadcasts make it look that way). If they hit it in the trees, no problem...just move the gallery around a bit and then thread the ball through that small opening.

There is quite a bit we can learn from watching the pros, but it's more in their routine, strategy, and overall demeanor on the course.

It pretty much stops there though. Keep in mind that these are the best players on the planet. They spend almost every day practicing for hours in order to execute difficult shots under immense pressure. Just because they make it look easy doesn't mean you should expect to be pulling off similar shots when you are playing.

There are so many golfers who get discouraged on the course when they chunk an iron on the fairway, or hit a drive out of bounds. They are under the impression that every shot they hit should be a great one. Part of that is because they are used to seeing the pros play golf in an effortless fashion.

If you are a recreational golfer looking to improve your game, the path to lower scores will be more about limiting mistakes than it will be about hitting great shots. This is a tough pill for most golfers to swallow because we all want to be hitting great shots out there.

Next time you screw up a few times on the course, don't get so down on yourself. You are supposed to do that; it's not your day job!

[43]

Fooled By False Golfing Promises

Commercials, articles, and all kinds of products that offer easy fixes constantly inundate golfers. If someone promises they can add 50 yards to your drives with one easy tip, it is probably too good to be true.

There are no shortcuts in golf, despite what you may have heard from people looking to take your hard-earned cash. That's not to say there are not useful products or teachers that can help you lower your scores, but they are usually not the ones making these outrageous claims.

The next time you are ready to pull out your credit card just remember that no one has the golfing Holy Grail. If they did, then they probably wouldn't need to advertise their product because it was so earth shattering. The golfing world wouldn't be able to stop talking about it!

[44]

Not Warming up Before a Round

If you have the opportunity to warm up, please take it. It can make a world of difference in your performance, especially on your earlier holes.

The most important thing to establish before your round is your feel in your putter and wedges. If you don't have that much time, these shots should be your main focus. Start with a few chip shots and work your way up to 1/2 - 3/4 wedge swings. These are the shots that require the most precision on the golf course (and might determine your score for the day). If you aren't properly warmed up it will be very difficult to get things going once your round starts.

If there is time for more work then you can make your way through the rest of your bag. Please don't fall victim to driver warm-ups. Swinging with just your driver will disrupt your tempo, and that's the last thing you want to bring to the first tee.

Another area you shouldn't ignore is the putting green. Establishing the speed of the greens is crucial, and will help prevent three putts during your round. Spend a few minutes putting from 20-30 feet away, and then focus solely on 4-6 footers so you can see the ball going in the cup to give you some positive mental feedback before you tee off.

A good warm up session is great for both your body and mind. The first few holes can be the most difficult if you haven't prepared yourself properly.

[45]

No Pre-Shot Routine

This is a big one, so pay attention.

The few seconds before you hit your shot can be a very nervous time for a golfer. One of the most effective ways to combat these jitters is to have a familiar routine.

A great pre-shot routine has three important elements:

1. It's deliberate and does not waste too much time.
2. You think about your target, and come up with a plan for your shot.
3. There is a trigger to signify to yourself you are ready to swing.

Here's an example of a routine that gets the job done.

After evaluating your distance you select your club. You stand behind your ball. You are thinking about the kind of shot you want to hit, and select a very specific target. You take two practice swings. While maintaining focus on your target, you address the ball and make sure you are aligned properly. You take one last look at your target, and then you slowly waggle the club backwards to remind yourself of your swing plane. Then you swing.

You don't have to do exactly the same thing in the example. Your trigger might be different, or you feel comfortable taking your practice swings next to the ball. Either way, come up with a routine that works for you and try to do it the same way every time before you hit a shot. The best way to do this is to incorporate it into your range sessions first.

There are so many times during a round where golfers are uncomfortable before their shots, and this is one of the easiest ways to solve that issue. Having a pre-shot routine that you are confident in, and can repeat, is one of the most important things any golfer can do to help themselves improve.

[46]

Ignoring Tempo

The golf world likes to talk about positions a lot. Where are your hands at the top of your swing? What does your takeaway look like?

While those can be important in solving a particular golfer's swing, an important fundamental that is almost never discussed is swing tempo. The one unifying theme between all great golfers is their tempo, and someone actually proved it.

John Novosel, the inventor of Tour Tempo, figured out that almost every single professional golfer of all time has a 3:1 ratio of the length of their backswing compared to their downswing. Their ability to repeat this tempo on every single swing is one of the main reasons why they are able to hit great shot after great shot. They have an internal clock that is synced perfectly.

Conversely, most amateur golfers struggle because their swings are generally too slow, and their tempo changes drastically from swing to swing. The theory is that when you are able to get your swing closer to the magic 3:1 ratio, and begin to repeat the same rhythm, a lot of the mistakes you were making in your swing start to disappear.

Simply put, solving your tempo can start improving the sequence of your swing, and all of a sudden your golf club will find a way into the right positions.

The reason tempo has largely been ignored by most teaching professionals is that there hasn't been a great way to measure it, or practice it.

There are three products that can help you with this:

1. The Tour Tempo tones, which you can purchase on your smart phone. These will allow you to sync up your swing to a series of beats that will help you improve your tempo.
2. Swing Analyzers: The newest models can track your actual tempo during your practice session, so you can track your progress.
3. The Orange Whip: This is probably the most successful swing trainer of all time, and it works. It allows golfers to feel a swing that is smooth and rhythmic. 10 minutes of training a day can go a long way.

Working on your tempo is wonderful because it doesn't occupy your mind with a ton of different swing thoughts or technical information. It is one of the most simple yet effective ways to improve your ability to repeat successful golf swings. Think about making it one of the focal points of your practice sessions.

[47]

Aiming at a General Area

You step up to the tee and hit your drive.

Wait, you forgot something! Did you pick a target to aim at? If it was the fairway, that's not specific enough.

Focusing your mind on a specific target before your shot is a very important step that most players aren't doing.

There is a long list of natural targets you can find on a golf course. It could be a tree in the background, a yardage marker, an undulation in the fairway, or a bunker in the distance. You can get creative with it.

Pick the target, commit to it, and focus on it during your pre-shot routine. If you lack this specific target, it will partially prevent you from committing to the shot.

This is a small mental tip that is easy to do that can become part of your routine. You may be surprised, but small changes like these can actually have a large impact on whether or not your shot will work out.

[48]

Not Using the Ol' Texas Wedge

The term "Texas Wedge" refers to using your putter anytime you are off the green, and many golfers aren't using this technique enough.

When you are faced with a situation where you are on the fairway or the fringe, and have a clear path to the green, it's sometimes a good idea to use your putter. You will see the pros doing it all of the time.

This is because your worst putt is going to be much better than your worst chip.

When you're not completely confident with a wedge in your hand, your margin of error on that particular shot can be quite high. You can chunk it, and leave the ball well short of the green. Or worse, you can skull it over the other side of the putting surface.

Both scenarios will leave you scrambling for your double bogey, which is not a good place to be as a golfer.

Conversely, from that same spot you can most likely get your ball on the green with your putter almost every time. A bad result could be a putt from 25-30 feet for par. That's much better than having a wedge in your hand for the next shot.

The Texas Wedge can be an effective tool at limiting double and triple bogeys, but will still give you a chance to save par. Try using it more on the course if you are not completely confident in your chipping technique off the green; there's no shame in it!

Playing the Ball Forward in Your Short Game

A vital element to a great short game is making solid contact every time. So many golfers waste shots around the green by hitting the ball way too heavy or too thin. It's incredibly frustrating to fail at getting the ball on the green from 20 feet away.

If you are playing the ball towards your lead foot...stop!

Dave Pelz has spent the better part of four decades studying golfers and their short games. He is one of the leading authorities on the game 100 yards and in.

He has found that one of the leading causes of mishits is ball position. Many golfers will move the ball up in their stance in an effort to hit a more lofted shot, but they sacrifice the ability to swing with proper technique.

You want the ball to be in a position where your swing bottoms out, and that is in the center of your stance. If you move it forward, then you will have to make adjustments with your arms, and will engage muscles in your body that should not be activated on shorter shots that require feel.

This is a simple fix that can save you a ton of strokes, and save you from some major frustration on the course. Keep the ball in the middle of your stance, or even a few inches towards the back.

[50]

Never Taken a Lesson

There are tons of ways to improve your golf game on your own time, and this book will give you plenty of ideas. However, there is a huge benefit to working with a teaching professional at some point.

It is always a good idea to have an experienced set of eyes take a look at your swing from time to time. A great pro can make small adjustments to your setup, grip, and swing plane that might fix major problems that have been plaguing you.

The most important thing is to find a teacher that suits your learning style.

Some pros are very technical, and certain students might not respond to that kind of teaching. There are also teachers who have a very distinct style of swing that they like to teach, but that might not suit your physical abilities.

There are two very important elements to a successful relationship with a pro:

1. Can they communicate the changes you need to make in a way you can understand?

2. Are you capable of making the adjustments they are suggesting?

If a student doesn't feel like they can answer both of those questions with a yes, then it is probably best to find someone else. The golf swing can be very complicated, and your time and money are best invested with someone who can work with your specific set of abilities. If not, then you might end up doing more harm to your game than good. You don't want to bring a swing out on the course that you don't feel good about.

[51]

Not Passing the Game On

There has been a lot written over the last few years about how golf is in decline, and the younger generation might not be interested in the game because it is too time consuming and difficult. Whether or not these predictions come true, it's incumbent on any golfer who truly loves the game to try and pass the game on.

This can be through your children, or even a brief encounter with a younger golfer at your local course. All golfers need to do everything they can to make sure the game we love lives on for future generations.

Golf is a special game that can teach children and young adults so many important lessons about life. Hard work, patience, mental fortitude, honor, respect...the list can go on forever. Let's do everything we can to make sure all of these important life lessons will continue to get passed on through this great game!

[52]

Misreading the Rough

If your ball has found the rough, the next decision you make is extremely important. One of the biggest mistakes most golfers make is not evaluating their lie in the rough properly. If you are too aggressive and do not anticipate how the clubface will react to your lie, you will ultimately compound your initial mistake.

The worst lies are the ones that can really destroy your hole if you don't play them properly. If your ball is mostly buried, this is where things can go very wrong. Longer rough has a tendency to grab the hosel of the club. This essentially means the ball can go almost anywhere (mostly to the left) if you are too aggressive with your swing.

The best thing to do on these nasty lies is to take your medicine, and try advancing the ball with a shorter club. When you swing with a shorter club like a pitching wedge, you naturally have a steeper angle of attack into the rough. This will allow you to make cleaner contact with the ball. You might not reach the green, but you will have avoided an even bigger mistake with this strategy.

Another tip that can be helpful out of the rough is checking whether or not the grass is growing against you, or with you. If you grass is growing with you, then you might get what is called a "flier," which means the ball might go further than you intended. Conversely, if the grass is growing against you, it will provide more resistance, and offer some of the same issues that arise with a deeply buried lie.

Taking the time to evaluate these lies and make a better decision can help avoid a huge mistake. A general rule of thumb to follow is to try and play the shot that you know can get you back to safety. Aggressiveness out of the rough is one of the biggest mistakes golfers make.

[53]

Thinking What Works in Other Sports Will Translate to Golf

Many people have arrived at golf from other sports. Once their childhood was over, their opportunity to play football, baseball, basketball and other sports had largely been ended. Golf offered an outlet for their competitive drive, and a way to use their body in an athletic way.

In almost every other sport you are asked to push your bodies to the brink, be aggressive, and above all, try as hard as you can.

Those are terrible pieces of advice for a golfer!

Aggressiveness leads to mental mistakes and large scores. Trying harder often results in body tension and poor swing performance. To play great golf you have to forget about all of those things that your coaches drilled into you as a child.

Being patient and working hard are two things that are certainly worth translating to golf from other sports. All of the other things that your coaches might have preached to you probably won't do you any good.

Golf is a unique game and requires a special set of skills to achieve success.

[54]

Range = Course

The practice range is a place to experiment with changes, and it can reveal your potential as a golfer.

A very common phrase spoken by golfers is, "I was hitting it so well on the range, and then I got on the course and all hell broke loose."

Some version of this conversation is going on right now on the 19th hole all around the world. Golfers are absolutely perplexed why they can't hit the same shots during a round as they do when they are practicing. It's extremely frustrating, and because our expectations are so out of line, it often results in ruining a round once we hit a few bad shots.

This is all simply because of pressure. When you go through a bucket of balls at the driving range, you're not usually worried about anything. You're just swinging away, and typically you remember all of the good shots you hit during your session.

During a round of golf you only have one chance to hit your shot. You haven't developed a rhythm by hitting a few practice shots before the one that actually counts, and you are faced with all kinds of obstacles that can clutter your mind with fear before you swing.

The best way to bring your driving range game onto the course is to practice with more purpose, and try to play games with yourself that will actually put some kind of pressure on whether or not you can execute the shot properly. Above all, don't be so hard on yourself! Just because you can hit a perfect drive on the range a few times does not mean you should expect to do the same thing every time you tee it up on the course.

[55]

Swinging for Power

We all want to hit the ball as far as we can. At the top of our swings there is a momentary pause, and then we attack. The problem most golfers have is that they are trying to add power to their game before they master two of the most important elements of the golf swing – tempo and balance.

The secret to hitting the ball farther is making solid contact as close to the sweet spot of the clubface as possible. If you're attempting to swing out of your shoes, it's going to be very difficult to do that.

When we watch professional golfers play, it almost looks like they are swinging without any effort, yet they can hit the ball enormous distances. It's because their swings have impeccable tempo, and they are striking the ball solidly almost every time.

If you want to hit the ball farther you have to start from the ground up. That means focusing on a smooth swing, and keeping your balance before you worry about swinging harder. Here's a drill on the driving range that can help you out.

Buy yourself some impact stickers; you can get them for less than $20 (or some of the other methods described earlier in the book). The next time you are at the driving range start using them and find out where exactly on the clubface you are making contact. Once you have established a baseline, it's time to move to the next step.

Your goal is to start making marks on the sticker as close to the center as possible. Swing at about 50% of your normal speed. Really focus on feeling the club throughout your swing, and keeping your balance. You will probably start hitting more shots closer to the sweet spot, and the feedback you get from this drill will help you figure out how the right swing will feel.

Once you become more proficient at striking the ball properly, then you can start adding more speed to your swing. A golfer who has an 85 mph swing can actually hit the ball farther than a player who is swinging 100mph. A lot of this has to do with where the ball is at impact on the clubface. Balance and tempo are the keys to solving this equation.

[56]

Declaring You've Got It Figured Out

The Golfing Gods are always watching over us. They offer little bits of encouragement when things aren't going well. It could be a perfectly struck shot at the end of a terrible round, or a birdie sandwiched between a bunch of double bogeys. These are the moments that always keep us coming back for more.

One thing is for certain. The second you declare that you have the game figured out, they will conjure up lightning bolts, and send them your way!

There's always a moment on the driving range or on the golf course where the game makes complete sense to us. You might have figured out a new swing move that is producing amazing results, or you've had your best round ever. These are the moments where we feel bullet proof, like we're never going to go through any bad times on the course again.

Eventually we'll be brought back down to earth, but it's probably best to understand the following statement in order to avoid major disappointment.

Golf is always changing on us, and we will never be able to conquer the game. This is part of why golf is so beautiful and frustrating at the same time.

Next time you have figured something out, or had a great round, try to take it in stride. There's nothing wrong with feeling good about your swing or the way you are playing... just don't ever tempt The Gods by thinking you've got it completely figured out.

[57]

Too Many Swing Tips at Once

There's always a guy at the driving range with a hot new swing tip. He is bragging about how it has changed his game completely, and of course 2-3 of his buddies are willing to listen as he shows them what he learned. Nobody ever stops to think where he got this tip, or if he is even qualified to be instructing other golfers about their swings.

Now everyone is trying to incorporate their version of the tip into their swing. It's spreading like a virus! Some who have listened to it might have a few good shots and declare this is the new swing for them, and get just as excited as their friend.

Fast-forward a week later...

They're all back on the range dejected and upset because they ended up shooting a terrible round when they were unable to incorporate this new swing change on the course.

This is a common story amongst golfers, and it's playing out on hundreds of golf courses as you read these words. Swing tips are a dime a dozen, and there is no shortage of people who are willing to dole them out. Since golf is such a difficult game, and we are all eternally searching for answers, players are more than willing to listen to anyone who has some advice for them.

The problem is that as a golfer you can only digest so much information at once. These tips might make sense when someone explains them to us, and we might be able to hit a few good shots on the range with them. But bringing them out on the course is an entirely different story.

It takes a lot of time and effort to make changes in your golf swing, and then trust them when the pressure is on. When you've only got one chance to hit that 7-iron, you might begin to doubt your new swing thought.

Instead of listening to all of these different tips and making constant changes, it's much better to make very minor adjustments. Do one at a time until it feels completely natural, and you can prove to yourself that it works in an actual round of golf. Then you can move on to the next one.

Your friend might have the best of intentions, but it might be smarter to stay put and keep working on your current swing, rather than constantly consuming these tips.

Think of it like being stuck in a traffic jam. Sometimes after you keep changing lanes, you realize you would have made it through more quickly if you just remained in the same one the whole time.

[58]

Speed Is Not Your Priority on Longer Putts

Avoiding three putts is very important in reaching your scoring milestones. This is exactly why speed should be your main focus on longer putts.

If you're standing over a putt that's longer than 15-20 feet, your chances of making it are unfortunately very small (it's less than 5%). Golfers who step up to these putts with the intention of making them will often become too aggressive with their stroke. Your goal on these putts is to keep the ball within a reasonable distance of the cup to make sure you are giving yourself an easy two putt.

Inside three feet is the magical number you want.

While the line is important on these putts, it's not crucial because you can still make the wrong read and leave yourself a stress-free tap in. Speed is where your attention should be focused.

There's no magic bullet to having great speed on the greens, but a few things will certainly help you. The first is practicing more. If you spend a portion of your time on the putting green, and working on your lag putting, your body will start to develop muscle memory, and you'll develop the feel of the distances.

One of the best ways to help with your speed on longer putts when you're on the course is to start walking the distance of the putt. This is another way to help your body feel the distance. As you address your ball and make your practice strokes, try to keep your eyes on the distance of the putt while you feel the length of stroke you are making with the putter.

It takes time and patience to develop your speed control, but the more you pay attention to it in your practice sessions and on the course, the more skilled you will become at keeping your putts closer to the hole.

[59]

Playing the Wrong Clubs

Golf equipment has come a long way over the last 20-30 years. While some manufacturers might exaggerate the benefits of their technology, it is still extremely important to play the right clubs for your game. If you have the money to invest, being fit by an experienced club maker can go a long way in improving your performance.

Not all clubs are made the same, and certain manufacturer's equipment might be better suited for your swing. Additionally, playing the proper shaft, and making sure the lie angle of your irons suits your swing can make a big difference. When you just show up to the store, and buy clubs without doing any kind of testing, you will possibly make the wrong decision.

Golf is a difficult game, and the last thing you want to do is make it harder for yourself by playing with the wrong equipment. Working with someone who is experienced can help you ensure that the money you invest in your next set is going to be well spent.

While you still have to put a good swing on the club no matter what, having confidence in your clubs can provide a huge mental boost to help you play your best golf. One caveat is not to give too much credit to the clubs, and constantly change which ones you are using because of poor play. The buck stops with the operator of the golf club, which is you!

[60]

Not Embracing the Sand

The bunker is one of the most frightening places for the recreational golfer. If you don't play the shot correctly then all kinds of terrible things can happen.

The reason why most players don't feel comfortable in the bunker is because they don't understand the correct way to play the shot. The good news is that it is not terribly complicated.

Your sand wedge is equipped with something called bounce, and this will help the club glide through the sand to help the ball "pop" out. You can only engage the bounce when you have the club face open, which is one of the biggest mistakes players make in the sand.

The correct way to play a bunker shot is to rotate the clubface completely open, and try to have an outside-to-inside swing path, so that the club remains open through impact to properly engage the bounce.

The next thing that most players forget about the sand is that it's the only shot in golf where you are not hitting the ball. If you watch a bunker shot in slow motion you will see that the club slides beneath the ball, and it propels the sand into the air along with the ball.

Golfers are so used to striking the ball first that their instinct is to do just that, which leads to the dreaded skulled bunker shot. You actually want to make contact a few inches behind the ball.

Next time you are in the bunker remember to keep the clubface open, and use the sand to "thump" the ball out.

[61]

Never Taken a Break From Golf

Everyone who has ever played this game has gone through a tough period where nothing seems to work out. Your swing is a mess, your scores have ballooned, and you are not enjoying your time on the course.

Some golfers will try to work harder through these issues. They'll spend more time on the range, and try to play even more. Unfortunately this ends up making things worse because sometimes you can't work your issues out this way.

Here's a piece of advice that you might think is crazy. Stop playing for a while, and take a break.

All golfers know what it is like to be down in the doldrums and feeling horrible about your game. When you take a few weeks off, or even a few months, it allows your mind and body to reset.

They always say that distance makes the heart grow fonder, and this can absolutely be the case with your golf game. A break from the game might make you change your perspective on things a bit, and make you appreciate your love for the game even more.

Additionally, time off can get some of those negative swing thoughts out of your head. When you return you might have a newfound appreciation for the game, and you will be more patient with yourself.

[62]

Not Reviewing Your Rounds

One of the greatest mistakes golfers make is that they don't use their on-course performance as a template for their practice sessions.

When a golfer has a terrible round, they often come away discouraged, and focus on all of the bad shots they hit in a negative light. They become convinced that they are just never going to be a great putter, or that they can't save par from off the green.

Unfortunately, it becomes a self-fulfilling prophecy, and the parts of their game that need the most amount of work get ignored in favor of the parts of the game where they feel comfortable.

There are now products such as GAME GOLF that can help track your rounds, and give you summaries of where your game is deficient. This data is a goldmine for golfers because we often don't know the truth about where we are losing strokes on the course.

We might assume that it's our performance off the tee, but when we really look into it, our wedges and putter might be the culprits.

Honesty, changing your habits, and analysis are the real ways to becoming better at this game. But without the proper information you won't know where to put in the work.

Start keeping track of your stats on the course, and really think about where you are losing strokes. These are the areas of the game where you should invest your practice time, rather than on your strengths.

[63]

Losing Focus After a Bad Shot

Your ball is sailing into the trees, and your stomach starts to sink. You yell out a four-letter word, and maybe your club takes a little bit of abuse.

All of a sudden your hands are sweating a bit and your pulse is racing. As you approach your ball you are still completely angry with yourself, and can't forgive the shot you just hit to get into this position. You step up to your ball in a rush, and hit an even worse shot than the one that got you there. You make the dreaded triple bogey, and the rest of your round is ruined.

The hardest thing to do as a golfer is to collect your thoughts after a bad shot. It's why some golfers end up gravitating towards shooting the same scores over and over again.

The reason you're not breaking 100, 90, or even 80 is not necessarily because you need a better swing. It's because you're not saving those crucial shots when things aren't going your way. If you can learn to slow your mind down, and focus on the big picture even when you're in trouble, that's the key to playing better golf.

Playing the aggressive shot is not the best decision. Usually that is our first instinct though. We want to fix the mistake we just made.

Taking your medicine and getting the ball back to safety is the smarter course of action. Losing one stroke to par instead of 3-4 on a hole is going to look a lot better 2 hours later!

The next time you hit a horrible shot on the course try and go through a mental exercise. Tell yourself that it is only one shot, and resist the urge to play an aggressive one. Keep telling yourself that you want to save as many strokes as possible wherever you can, and try your best to maintain your focus.

This is much easier said than done, but being able to sharpen your mental game is a guaranteed way to become a better golfer.

[64]

Playing Lofted Wedge Shots Too Often

There is a time and a place for the lofted shot in your pitching and chipping, but it's certainly not on every shot. A common mistake of the average golfer is trying to fly the ball too high around the green.

If you are looking to lower your scores, one of the fastest ways to do it is to become more effective in your short game. This is an area where golfers can throw away a ton of strokes quickly. Keeping the ball as low as possible, and letting your chips and pitches run out like putts will help limit your mistakes.

When you keep the ball on the ground you have a much lower margin of error.

Playing lofted shots are more difficult to pull off, and require a great deal of skill. When you mess up these shots you might fail to reach the putting surface, or leave yourself very long putts that will result in double bogeys.

Keeping the ball lower will minimize these errors. You want to give yourself a chance at making par, but you also want to make sure you're not scrambling to make a bogey either. Next time you are on the course try to roll the ball out more by using less-lofted clubs.

[65]

Standing Too Close or Far Away From the Ball

There are many minor adjustments that golfers can make that will unlock great potential in their ball striking. Sometimes we will alter our posture and the way we address the ball over time without even realizing it. That is why Jack Nicklaus would meet with his swing coach after every winter to have a checkup on how he was aligned.

Even the smallest of changes can alter how well we hit the ball.

One of these small fixes is how far you are standing from the ball. There is no one-size-fits-all solution to this, meaning there isn't a proper distance for all golfers. It all depends on your swing plane, and a few other factors. Overall, you want to give yourself the best chance of making proper contact with the ball with your setup and posture.

One of the best ways to figure this out for yourself is to simply let your hands fall into a comfortable position. If you are too close to the ball then your hands might be way too upright, or propped up. Conversely, if you are too far your hands might be way too low, and your body is hunched over a bit. It's always best to have a trained eye take a look at your setup because sometimes it's difficult to feel where you actually are.

The next time you are at the range, experiment with small changes in your ball position to see if something clicks. If you are crowding the ball, having it a few inches further away might allow you to swing more freely. This is an easy thing to experiment with that won't alter your swing too much.

Sometimes the answers to our problems are this simple.

[66]

Swing Vanity

One of the biggest myths in golf is that you need to have a beautiful, fundamentally sound swing in order to shoot lower scores. This couldn't be further from the truth, for numerous reasons.

A majority of the best players in the world have perfect looking swings, but even in their ranks there are quite a few golfers who have made it to the promised land without having a cookie-cutter tour swing. The reason why players with unconventional swings can succeed is because they trust what they are doing, and can repeat it.

The only thing you should be concerned about with your golf swing is if you can get the ball headed in the vicinity of where you are aiming. If you can do that with decent regularity, you've conquered a big part of the battle.

Stop thinking you need to be hitting certain hand positions, or trying to mimic a certain tour player's swing. Your golf swing is your unique fingerprint, and you should be proud of it! Rather than making sweeping changes that are uncomfortable to your body, you should try to work with what you've got, and make small changes here and there.

If you can repeat a move (no matter how weird it might look) that gets the ball headed to your target, then stick with it. You will never trust a swing on the golf course that isn't right for you.

[67]

Never Played a Match Against Friends

Golf can be a lonely game if you're only keeping your own scores all of the time. If you can get a good foursome together, it's fun to get a little wager going and try out a few different formats.

It will make things a little more interesting and will keep you interested in the whole round, even if you have a bad stretch of holes.

Here are five formats you can try out with friends:

NASSAU

This is by far the most popular game out there. Here are the rules:

There are three separate bets in a Nassau. There is a match for the front 9, back 9, and overall 18 holes. Most people will wager the same dollar amount on each leg, or sometimes assign a larger amount to the 18-hole match. It's a great game that keeps both teams interested throughout the entire round because of the various legs.

Variations: The variation most golfers like are with "dots." Each team receives a dot for a birdie, closest to the pin on a par 3, or a bunker save. You assign a dollar amount for each dot, and at the end of the round the team with more dots gets paid out on the difference. If your team had 17 dots and the opponent had only 9 dots, you would win $8 if you had agreed that they were worth one dollar each. Some people like to play with presses, which is a double or nothing bet if you are down by over 2 holes or more. They can be optional or automatic.

SKINS

This is probably the second-most popular game, and the rules are pretty straightforward. Each hole is assigned a dollar amount, or a skin. For example, if you were playing $2 skins the most you could lose is $36. The kicker here is the carryovers. If you end up tying on any holes, the skins carry over. So you could be left with a hole that is worth $10 if you had tied the previous 4 holes...that's where things get interesting!

VEGAS

This one isn't for the faint of heart. Things can get real ugly in Vegas (don't we know it).

In Vegas, the scores of each player on a team are paired, and then matched up against the other team. For example, if you scored a 4 and your partner scored a 6 you would have a 46. If the other team had a 5 and a 6, they would score a 56. Therefore, your team would win 10 points on that hole.

Some people will play $1 for each point, so this can end up being a game for really heavy gamblers. You can assign a nickel, dime, or quarter for each point to make it more reasonable. Some people also cap the losses at 10 points for each hole.

WOLF

Wolf is fun because you are constantly changing playing partners, and you're out for yourself overall.

Before the match starts you establish a playing order. This will rotate each hole, with the next player in order having honors. On each hole the player teeing off last is the "wolf." The wolves can either choose to go at it themselves, and take on all 3 golfers, or choose a partner for the hole.

If you choose a partner it must be immediately after their tee shot. For example, if the second group member hits a great drive you have to choose right then, and can't wait for the 3rd player to hit their shot. You then play the hole as a best ball format, and the lowest score from each team determines who wins the hole.

If the wolf decides he doesn't like any of the tee shots he can elect to play the hole 1 vs. 3. In that instance the points are doubled. At the end of the round you tally up each player's points to see who is winning what. Sometimes people will determine beforehand a pot that is won by first and second place. Or you could pay out based on a dollar amount assigned to points.

SIXES (HOLLYWOOD & ROUND ROBIN)

This is another popular format because you are changing teams within the round a few times.

There are three separate six-hole matches in this format, and you team up with a different partner on each leg. You can play any format you want on each match, but most people like to play a best ball match. Your goal is to win 2 out of 3 of the matches.

The next time you play a round with your friends, try out one of these games. Make sure the stakes are reasonable so that nobody is yelling and screaming at the end of the day!

[68]

Misalignment

If you're not aimed in the right direction, golf can become a much more difficult game. The pros are constantly working on their aim, and you will often see them practicing with alignment rods on the range. If this is a major concern for them, then it should be for you.

This book is filled with small tips that can help lower that number at the end of your round. This is an important one.

If you were to follow the average golfer during a round, and show them where they are actually aimed versus where they think they are aimed, most of them would be shocked. They might believe that their feet and shoulders are pointing at the green, but in reality they are aimed at the trees about 25 yards right of the pin.

Over time our alignment can drift off line without us realizing it. We start becoming comfortable with a different posture in our bodies. This is exactly why you should always use some kind of alignment drill on the range to make sure you are not forming any bad habits.

Alignment rods are an inexpensive product to help fix this problem, or you could even use one of your clubs. Before you address the ball make sure they are pointed at your target, and then you can settle in to your stance, and use them as a visual aid to make sure your body is pointing in the right direction.

Going through this process will improve your ability to make sure you are aimed properly during a round. You can't hit the ball towards your target if your alignment is off.

[69]

Not Using a GPS or Rangefinder

There's no longer an excuse not to use a yardage device on the golf course. They have come down in cost significantly, and the benefit they can provide to your game is tremendous.

Golfers have plenty of things to fill their heads with doubt before they swing a club. Anything they can do to remove some of those doubts will result in better swings on average.

One of those worries should not be, "I hope I have the right club."

You need to be confident in the club you select on each shot, and a lot of that has to do with your yardages. One part of that equation is being honest with how far you can hit your irons, and the second part is knowing the actual yardage. If you guess how far it is to clear the water hazard, or to reach the front of a green, you probably won't make a confident swing.

One of the best investments a golfer can make is buying a GPS or Rangefinder. A GPS is probably the best solution for most golfers because it can instantaneously give you yardages to the front, center, and back of the green. Sometimes when players use a rangefinder they will fixate to the yardage of the pin, and that might not be the best target for them.

You can now get a GPS device for under $100 that will come preloaded with almost every golf course in the world. It's certainly worth the money.

[70]

Thinking the Term "Course Management" Is a Job Title

Course management refers to your strategy during your round, and has nothing to do with managing the operations of an actual golf course.

Having the right course management strategy can save you a TON of strokes, and is probably the most overlooked skill by golfers. Your strategy on your tee shots, approach shots, and all other facets of golf is one of the key elements in determining how well you will play on any given day.

It requires a great deal of discipline, but being a good course manager is all about staying in the moment. Here are a few examples of great course management:

- Choosing a club other than driver off of the tee when you know it is a tight fairway, and you want to give yourself the best chance of staying in the fairway.

- Favoring the side of the green situated away from trouble regardless of where the pin is located.

- Punching your ball safely back into the fairway rather than trying to thread it through three sets of trees.

Most low-handicap golfers are great course managers, and it's a vital element missing from the average golfer's game. Your brain is sometimes the most important club in the bag.

What can you do to become a better course manager?

The first step is being realistic with yourself and your abilities. Most players are way too aggressive with their targets and club selections. Before you hit your shot ask yourself a very simple question, "what is the shot I can pull off most of the time?"

If it's not hitting the ball over the water hazard 180 yards away, maybe it's a better idea to lay up.

The best course managers are always thinking and analyzing. It's quite similar to great poker players who can instantly calculate their odds of various hands when the cards come out.

If you start paying more attention to this part of the game, you will begin to eliminate some of the costly mistakes that result in double and triple bogeys.

[71]

Can't Smell the Roses

There are so many players who spend the 4-5 hours a week they get to play golf in a grumpy mood. They are unhappy during their rounds starting with a bad tee shot. Unfortunately they lose sight of the fact that golf is a privilege, not a chore.

There aren't many other games that you can play for life, spend time outdoors, and share with your friends like you can with golf. We all get caught up in trying to conquer the game and shoot our best scores that we forget that golf is supposed to be fun.

The next time you are out on the course try to remember this, even if you're not playing well. Golf is not a walk spoiled, it's a gift!

[72]

Developing Technique, and Not Skill

Technique is important in golf, and refers to the fundamental execution of your golf swing. Many players will spend a lot of time working on their technique, and it's certainly time well spent. Having good technique is the backbone of a good golfer.

However, having skill might be even more important. Skill refers to your ability to adapt technique in unfamiliar circumstances.

Hitting golf balls on the range helps develop your technique. It's a controlled environment. You are getting the same lie on the mat every time, and there are no obstacles such as trees or hazards to make you think about how to alter your shot.

However, when you get on the golf course, things change. You are faced with different lies, uneven stances, and a combination of obstacles. This is where skill becomes important.

For example, you might have hit your ball into some trees, and in order to get the ball safely back on the fairway you'll to have to hit a low punch shot that will curve a little bit from right to left. That's probably not something you have practiced on the driving range, and you will have to adapt your technique in order to execute the shot. For a player who has not developed much skill this will be difficult to pull off.

So how do you develop skill? You need to start practicing outside of the box a little bit. A great example would be work you can do with your wedges in a backyard or an open field. If you have 10 balls, you can try to hit them all to the same target, with varying trajectories. Start experimenting with how you manipulate the clubface (open or closed), where the ball is in your stance, and give yourself all different types of lies to work with.

The point is if you keep practicing shots that are under perfect conditions, you'll never develop any skill as a golfer. The next time you are at a range try imagining that a tree is in front of you, and figure out a way to curve the ball around it. Imagine there's a bunker right in front of you, and you have to hit a lofted shot over it to land it on the green safely. Get creative!

A round of golf can throw so many different scenarios at you, and your ability to adapt your technique is one of the most important tools for a golfer. That is why skill is so important.

[73]

Forgetting About Wind and Elevation Change

You've struck your 7-iron perfectly. You're holding your pose, and watching the ball track towards the pin, expecting it to drop 2 feet from the hole. To your shock and dismay the ball lands 25 yards short in the bunker.

Wait, what just happened???

You forgot to factor a few things into your club selection. Did you notice that the green was elevated a little bit? Did you take into account that the wind was into your face?

Many times golfers get their yardage, step up to their ball, and just hit it. They don't take time to think about the factors that will affect how far their ball will fly. Having a feel for elevation changes and wind takes time to develop, but it's one of the necessary course-management skills a golfer needs.

If you are playing the same course most of the time, start making mental notes on which holes feature major elevation changes. A steep incline, or drop in elevation, can change your distance by as much as two to three clubs. Try to keep track of the wind as well. If your course has trees you can take a look at the top of them to see which direction the wind is blowing, or you could toss up some grass before you make your swing.

The point is you want to get as much information as possible before you commit to your shot. If you just make a swing without considering any of these factors you're not giving yourself the best chance for success.

[74]

Swaying

A common mistake amongst golfers is that they "sway" away from the ball during their backswing. Instead of remaining mostly centered over the ball (some movement is OK), their torso will move backwards quite a bit during their swing. This leads to their body getting stuck behind the ball at impact, which makes it difficult to hit quality golf shots.

The best way to fix this is to focus on rotating from your hips, or pivoting your body during your swing. This is one of the secrets of a powerful and effective golf swing. You want your body to coil rather than sway.

Some people might have difficulty making a complete rotation like you see the pros doing, but even a little more pivot can help your swing out, and prevent you from becoming The Leaning Tower of Pisa.

Losing Confidence After One Bad Round

There's probably nothing worse in this world than the crushing feeling of defeat after having a disastrous round of golf. It can bring you to your lowest lows, and have people in your life who don't play questioning why you would even subject yourself to such torture.

Some days things are not going to work out on the golf course no matter what we do. If you watch the pros on TV you know that it can happen to them all of the time. Even their confidence can get rocked after a bad round, and send them into a tailspin of bad play for a few weeks, or even months.

Golf is disproportionally a mental game, and our confidence in ourselves is one of the main determining factors on how well we will play on any given day. Every golfer has reached a point where one round has them staring into the abyss, and questioning whether they will ever play well again, or if they even want to continue playing at all.

Don't jump.

The other side of the coin is that you're always one round away from a spectacular performance on the course. Golf has a way of punishing our egos when we fly too high, and then offering gifts of encouragement when we think things can't get any worse. If you can remain positive in your darkest golfing hours, things will come up smelling roses once again. That's a guarantee!

Just try and remember that nothing is permanent in golf.

[76]

No Golf Library

I hope you're enjoying the book so far. Hopefully you've had fun reading it, and picked up a ton of useful tips at this point. A lot of what I have learned about the game has been from some of the great golfing minds. Here is a list of books that I consider required reading for any golfer looking to get better:

Harvey Penick's Little Red Book by Harvey Penick

Ben Hogan's Five Lessons: The Modern Fundamentals of Golf by Ben Hogan

Golf is Not a Game of Perfect by Dr. Bob Rotella

The Short Game Bible by Dave Pelz

Unconscious Putting by Dave Stockton

Fearless Golf by Dr. Gio Valiante

The Practice Manual by Adam Young

Golf My Way by Jack Nicklaus

Zen Golf: Mastering the Mental Game by Joseph Parent

There are so many ways to learn to play golf effectively. I believe each of these authors have created works that are easy to understand, and feature real advice that will help you gain some new perspective on the game.

This is a well-rounded list that features help on the technical side as well as the mental side. All of these authors have helped improve my game, and they certainly can help yours.

[77]

You Are Hungry and Thirsty

Playing 18 holes of golf is actually more of a physical activity than most people realize. Just like any other sport, you want to make sure you are properly hydrated and have enough energy to perform well.

It's very difficult to play golf when you're light-headed and hungry.

Always make sure you have enough water to last your entire round, and more importantly keep a few snacks in your bag. Processed foods that are high in sugar usually aren't the best choice. A hot dog and beer at the turn isn't the best idea either. It might be smarter to save that for the 19th hole.

The easiest things to bring along are fruits like bananas, oranges, and apples. They will give you a nice jolt of energy without having a crash a few holes later. Nuts are a great source of energy too, and will keep you feeling full for most of your round.

It's best to plan ahead, and try to bring your snacks and water with you from home. Most courses don't have the healthiest options, and will charge you quite a bit more than your grocery store.

[78]

The Fidgets

There are many golfers who are on a dance floor before they swing, and can't stop fidgeting. They are so uncomfortable over the ball and can't commit to their shot. One of the most common errors that occurs as a result of this is they end up aiming in a completely different direction than where they initially intended.

If you are a chronic shuffler before your shots, be mindful of what is happening with your feet. You might be shifting your target angle without even realizing it.

Establishing a pre-shot routine can help with this. If this is a problem for you make sure that one of your mental cues during your routine is to set your feet, and commit to maintaining your position before you swing.

[79]

Worrying More About Your Score Rather Than How to Lower It

Golfers are notorious score chasers. We're all guilty of this in most rounds we play. Somewhere in the back of our heads we have a number in mind that will make us thrilled. Unfortunately, it usually represents an above-average performance. The second we feel we might have blown our chances at achieving this score, the round begins to slip away.

While it is hard not to focus on what scores we're shooting all of the time, the best way to improve your scores is actually to not worry about them so much.

This sounds counterproductive, but if you can keep yourself focused on the process rather than the results, you will start to see improvement.

Golfers are often lost on how to improve their games. Their default activity is to run over to the range and hit a bucket of balls. The answers are right in front of you though; you just have to pay attention to your game.

Every round of golf should offer you a clue on where you should be putting your work in. Are you three putting quite often? Do you miss most of your fairways? Did you get up and down for par at all?

Rather than being disappointed with the score you just shot, start looking for these clues in your game, and use them as a blueprint on where you need to spend your practice time. If something is a glaring weakness, your goal should be to devote most of your time there, rather than practicing parts of the game you might already be proficient at.

If you keep doing the same things over and over again, your scores are never going to improve. Most golfers feel that they might be entitled to a certain score because they have played the game long enough, or they think they might have put in enough practice time.

Golf can be a brutal game, and it owes you nothing. If you can start being a bit more analytical about your game, and stop your obsession with your scores, then they just might drop!

[80]

Wrong Angles on the Tee Box

How you align yourself on the tee box is very important, and golfers often don't set themselves up for success. If you watch professional players you will see that they sometimes choose one side of the tee box. This is because they want to give themselves enough room for their ball flight.

If you play a fade, you want to tee it up on the right-hand side, and vice versa for a draw. This gives the ball enough room to make its turn.

If you are playing a left to right ball flight, and teed it up on the left hand side of the tee box, then you really haven't made enough room for the ball to turn back into the fairway.

Using the correct alignment strategy based on your typical ball flight is much more important than most players think, and it gives you a better chance of keeping the ball in play off the tee.

[81]

Too Many Swing Thoughts

If you are thinking about more than 2-3 things before you swing a golf club, you will probably be in trouble. It's very difficult to make a fluid golf swing when you are worrying about your takeaway, hand position at the top of your swing, your knee turn, shoulder turn...well, you get the point.

The best golf swings are made with very simple thoughts, like "smooth" or "stay balanced." Taking a checklist of thoughts out to the golf course is going to paralyze you. That's often why players who have just taken a lesson will have a terrible round afterwards. They have a new thought that they are trying to work on, and it's very difficult for it to feel natural when the pressure is actually on (compared with the practice range).

Your goal as a golfer is to get to a place where you aren't thinking about too many things during your swing. If you can keep your focus on 1-2 key thoughts you will allow a good swing to happen, rather than trying to force it.

[82]

Fearing Your Bad Shots

Golf is a game of mistakes. There is no way around this, and as much as we try to ignore this fundamental part of the game, we will inevitably hit some terrible shots during our rounds.

Most of the time we have it completely backwards. We are fearing our mistakes, and almost waiting for them to happen. You might have made it to the 5th hole without a major blunder, but in the back of your mind you are thinking, "when is it coming??" Sure enough, shortly afterwards the dreaded mishit arrives and your mind is spiraling out of control, and you might be in a complete panic that your round is coming to an end.

It's OK, it was bound to happen!

If more golfers would embrace these mistakes, rather than fear them, they could improve their performance greatly. The next time you are on the course, and you've hit a terrible shot, try taking a deep breath. Remind yourself that you were supposed to hit that shot, and that no golf round would be complete without a few big mistakes.

Too many golfers assume that their round is going to be a straight line, and as soon as they veer off of that line they start to lose control, get angry, or panic.

Golf is anything but a straight line, and if you can embrace all of the twists and curves that are going to happen during your round, you will become a much better player.

[83]

You Have No Feel

Harvey Penick was a huge proponent of feel in a golfer's short game. If given the choice between having better feel or technique, he always sided with a golfer who had better feel. He was one of the wisest golfing minds ever, so this is advice worth listening to.

There is no doubt that having the right technique with your pitching, chipping, and putting will help you become a better golfer. It's a huge piece of the complex puzzle that is golf. However, without feel, you are completely lost on those shots.

So what is feel?

Feel is throwing a football the right trajectory to hit your receiver in stride. It is hitting the perfect drop shot in tennis that your opponent can't run down.

No instructor in the world can properly teach feel to a golfer, but you can point him or her in the right direction on how to develop it. It has to be achieved through repetition and experimentation.

In golf, we use the club to advance the ball, and it's much harder to develop this necessary skill. The golf swing is nothing like throwing a ball, which is why so many golfers have a hard time developing feel, and even understanding it.

Feel is a golfer's best friend, and can get him or her out of almost any situation. You can find it, lose it, and then get it back again. In other words, you always need to be working on it, and you certainly never have it completely conquered.

The only surefire way to get feel in your golf game is to be working on it. You can do this by honing in on a certain distance, and then testing yourself with random ones.

For example, if you're working on your chipping you could take ten balls and work on hitting the ball at one specific target. When you feel like you have become proficient, you can test yourself by picking five different targets and see how close you can get the ball each time.

If you can start to develop feel in your short game, things will become much easier for you on the golf course.

[84]

Passing the Buck

Golfers love to place the blame elsewhere. The wind caused their shot to come up short. The greens were not rolling true. The group in front of them was playing too slow. Someone could write a whole encyclopedia on excuses from golfers, and every single one of us could make a meaningful contribution.

There's no doubt that there are many things beyond our control during a round of golf. Our ball can land in a divot, or our putt could hit a spike mark on the green. However, focusing on all of these things and letting them bring you down is holding you back from playing your best golf.

A favorite pastime of golfers is to give a recap of their rounds, and talk about all of the things that prevented them from shooting the score they wanted to.

"If I didn't put it in the water on 14, I probably would have broken 90."

Well the ball did go in the water. You hit it there!

Most great golfers don't make excuses for their play. They think about their mistakes, and try to improve on them. They are the ones who are usually the most quiet during these pity parties.

If you find you are the type of golfer who is constantly making excuses for your poor play that don't include the words "me" or "I" in them, then maybe it's time to take a step back and think about what you could be doing to prevent these mistakes.

There is no such thing as an easy golf course. The game is inherently challenging even in the most benign setups. Just keep in mind that you are the one who determines your score, not the course.

[85]

The Quick Transition

The average golfer's swing is like the biggest roller coaster at the amusement park. It's a slow climb to the top, and then all hell breaks loose. The club is speeding to the ball with reckless abandon as it plummets to the bottom.

Your golf swing should not be like this. It should be more like the roller coaster for the kids under 8, smooth and controlled.

Our instinct at the top of our swing is to attack the ball in an effort to hit it long and straight. If you can resist this temptation, and focus on maintaining a smooth tempo throughout your entire swing, you will reduce the amount of errant shots you hit throughout a round.

The best golfers in the world don't swing hard, they swing smooth. Be patient with the golf club, it will get to the ball eventually.

[86]

Frequent Temper Tantrums

Tempers and golf do not mix well. There is no quicker way to guarantee a bad round than by losing your composure on the course. Additionally, no one wants to be around a player who is tossing clubs and expletives everywhere.

We all struggle with our reaction to bad shots, and sometimes our frustrations can boil over. You want to play your best, and if things don't work out it's certainly understandable to get angry.

There is a fine line though. If you're the player who is constantly letting your temper get the best of you on the course, then you might need to take a step back and think about things. Why are you playing if you can't enjoy the game? Is it worth it?

Golf can be one of the most important things in our lives, but we have to make sure we are enjoying our time on the course first. Sometimes it's good to take a step back from the game if you are struggling with your anger issues.

Remember, it's just a game and the primary reason you are supposed to be playing it is to enjoy yourself. If your blood pressure is off the charts during a whole round of golf, then you might need to dramatically change your expectations of what you want from the game, and how you should be playing it.

[87]

Believing Distance Alone Will Lower Your Scores

It's hard for a golfer not to associate distance with lower scores these days. Every commercial, new product, and training device talks about how it is going to add distance to your game. There are also stats that actually show hitting the ball farther will lead to lower scores.

If you go to any driving range after working hours you'll see stalls filled with golfers trying to hit their drivers as far as humanly possible. By the way most golfers devote their practice time, you would think a round of golf required you to use the driver 90% of the time, and your score was a reflection of total yards carried!

Hitting the ball farther can make golf much easier. Having a pitching wedge in your hand is much better than a 5-iron, but that's only if your ball is in play.

In your quest to hit the ball farther you're possibly ignoring another key element, which is accuracy. If you can't add distance with reasonable accuracy, then it will all be a waste of time unfortunately. In other words, your scores will not drop just because you are able to hit your driver further.

This is another part of the game where you have to be honest with yourself. If you are able to add another 5-10 yards to your shots it can be a tremendous advantage. Just try to be aware of how that distance might relate to whether or not your ball is landing in a spot where you can safely play your next shot.

[88]

Ignoring Gadgets

There are a ton of new products that have come on the market over the last few years that can really help golfers improve their games. They include GPS systems, swing analyzers, and game-tracking devices.

While most of these devices are not the quick fixes for your game that some companies make them out to be, they can provide great insight on where you need to spend your practice time, and help you make better decisions on the course. Data can be a golfer's best friend if it is used properly, and most players can get some help from a few of these products.

Here are three examples of how some of these gadgets can help you:

GPS - Do you know how many players are leaving shots on the course because they don't know their actual yardages to the front, center, and back of the greens? This information is vital in selecting the right club, and you should be taking it into account before each shot.

Game tracking devices - Systems like GAME GOLF can analyze all of the shots you are hitting on the golf course, and give you personalized suggestions on how to fix your game. If you find out that after 10 rounds you are losing most of your strokes to par because your scrambling stats are far worse than a golfer who shoots your target score, then maybe that will finally convince you to start practicing with your wedges and putter more!

Swing Analyzers - Some of the newest products on the market can take a look at your swing and offer personalized suggestions on how to fix it. More importantly you can track your results over time, and see how much progress you are making. This is a way to add more purpose to your practice sessions.

Technology on its own will not help your golf game, but if used effectively it can make you a more efficient golfer.

[89]

Practicing Without Purpose

Golfers often wonder why they can't bring the shots they are hitting on the range out to the course. It has to do with the fact that they are not properly focusing their mind when they practice.

In order to become a professional in many fields, you have to complete some form of on-job training. Commercial pilots will log hundreds of hours on simulators. Surgeons will practice on cadavers. Electricians will have to be an apprentice for a couple of years.

The point is that in order to become proficient in these fields you have to practice by simulating scenarios that will occur when you are actually performing the job. While golf is not our profession, a similar attitude can work for your golf game.

This is where most golfers fall short in their practice sessions. They will show up to the range and hit a bucket of balls without giving much thought to what they are doing. They hit the same club over and over again, which does not really simulate what is happening on a golf course. It's one of the main reasons why so many players never improve.

In order to make the most out of your practice sessions you have to have a goal in mind, and really think about what you are trying to accomplish. One of the best ways to do this is playing games with yourself, and thinking about areas of the game where you need help.

Maybe in your last few rounds you weren't able to get up and down for par at all. Well maybe it's time to practice a few different distances with your wedges. Challenge yourself, and see if you can accomplish some kind of goal like hitting your target 5 times in a row. Anything you can do to put pressure on yourself during your practice time will help you when you are out on the course.

The next time you are at the range, try to think a little bit more about each shot. Give it meaning. Ask yourself what your target is.

If you just hit a 7-iron, switch over to a driver. Keep changing things up to give yourself a mental reboot before each swing, because that's what it is like on the actual course.

[90]

Scooping Your Chips

One of the cardinal sins of all golfers when they go to pitch or chip around the green is that they do not maintain a proper wrist angle, and they end up "scooping" the ball. This costs golfers around the world countless strokes, and many wedges get tossed across greens when this happens.

One of the easiest ways to focus on making proper contact with your wedges around the green is to keep your hands ahead of the club through impact. The best way to describe this technique is called the "Hinge and Hold". While this isn't the only way to chip effectively, it has proven to be one of the easiest methods for golfers of all levels to master over the years.

The idea is to get your wrists hinged quickly, and hold them in the same position through impact. When you lose this angle, and your hands end up behind the clubface at impact, this is where trouble happens.

It's a simple concept to understand, but requires some practice to make it feel natural. This is almost a foolproof way to make sure you are making crisp contact with the ball, and it will save you a ton of strokes over your rounds.

Whether or not you choose this method to chip, you want to adopt a technique that you can repeat, and will limit your mistakes around the green. So many players throw away shots because they haven't mastered one specific technique around the greens, and they always try to execute a different type of shot every time.

Pick one, and be really good at it.

[91]

Never Practiced on a Course

There is one kind of practice that can really accelerate your progress, and it happens on the actual golf course.

Throwing a few balls down on the course during your walk can be extremely effective because it's the closest thing you'll ever get to a live round of golf.

The pros always have special access to the course before the tournament, and you will see them spending time on different parts of each hole practicing their putting, chipping, or other wedge play.

If you can find a similar situation for yourself, this is a great opportunity to work on your game and not worry about your score at all. Take about 3-4 balls, and work on all kinds of different shots.

You can only do this kind of practice if you are by yourself, or with another player who is trying to do the same. Of course if you see anyone behind you, make sure you are not holding him or her up, or perhaps waive him or her through. This is not always possible on certain courses, but the best time to do it is either very early in the morning, or just before dusk.

[92]

Convincing Yourself a Shot Is Not Going to Work Out

This is a tough one, but it is extremely important. Your mental state before you hit a shot is extremely important. One of the most common errors golfers make is that they convince themselves a shot is not going to work out before they even hit it.

We all do it, and it's one of the most common mistakes.

The best golfers are positive thinkers. They never get too down on themselves, and always try to focus on the shot at hand. If they don't feel confident taking driver off the tee, they will use another club. If the opening in the trees doesn't make them feel comfortable, then they will just pitch out on to the fairway, and take their medicine.

If you know a shot is too hard to play, and you've already thought to yourself "I'm gonna go for broke on this one," then things probably won't work out for you.

Commitment is the most important thing before any swing happens. If you are not committed to the shot you are about to play then you either need to take a few extra seconds to collect your thoughts, or think about playing a different club or target that makes you feel more comfortable.

[93]

You Are Not Honest With Yourself

Honesty can mean a lot of things in golf. It can relate to your score, your abilities, or even what you want out of the game.

If you aren't being honest with your scores, you are just cheating yourself.

If you aren't honest with your abilities, you will have more shots end in failure.

If you're not honest with what you want out of golf, then you probably won't enjoy the game much.

Golf is a game that rewards honesty in different ways. If you start being more honest, then you will become a more successful golfer.

[94]

Peaks and Valleys With Your Emotions

18 holes of golf is a really long time. If you're unfortunate enough to get stuck on a slow course, it might take as long as six hours. During that time there are so many things that can occur, often leading to a roller coaster of emotions.

There are all kinds of golfers out there in terms of emotions. There are hot heads, stoics, jokers, and the list can go on. Your particular emotional makeup as a golfer is certainly unique to you, but there is one general mistake that many golfers make that holds them back from playing better.

Every shot you hit on the course is a new opportunity, and your ability to put what happened on your previous shot behind you is an extremely important skill. That's exactly why it's best to avoid any kind of major outburst of joy or anger. It's often difficult to calm yourself down by the time you are ready to hit your next shot.

That's not to say you should be completely vanilla out there. In fact it does help to pump yourself up a little bit after you sink a putt, or let off a little bit of steam after a terrible drive. You just don't want to get all the way to 10/10 on the emotional meter. Maybe a 5 or 6 would be more appropriate.

The steadier you can be with your emotions, the more prepared you will be to focus on your next shot.

You can certainly file this away in the "easier said than done category." Having this kind of control is a skill that is no different than being able to chip properly. You need to work on it over time.

[95]

Playing Too Much, or Not Enough

There is a fine balance between practicing, and being on the course enough to be comfortable. Golfers are usually at one extreme. They either play all of the time and don't spend any time practicing, or most of their time is spent at the driving range without much live action.

We all have limitations on how much we can do of either, but your game is usually going to be sharpest when you can keep a balance between the two. Your practice sessions are a time to work on the parts of your game that are deficient in your rounds. Your time on the course is to test your preparation.

The two feed off each other, and if you are spending too much on one side, then your game might suffer. Trying to keep this balance is important, and you should be mindful of the two.

[96]

Hitting a Shot Without a Plan

The golf ball will not magically go where you want it to if you hastily step up and make a swing without giving it much thought.

Did you consider all of your distances? Did you think about what side of the green you should favor based on the trouble surrounding it? Did you think about what club selection off the tee was going to give you the best chance of keeping the ball in play?

Golf is a game of strategy. Your goal is to limit your mistakes as much as it is to hit great shots. This is why every shot needs to have a plan. This will help you stay in the moment and prevent some of the major mistakes that destroy your round.

Before you step up to your shot just ask yourself one simple question: "What's my plan here?"

It might surprise you, but taking the time to go through that small mental exercise will save strokes during a round. Better golfers are always thinking about the purpose of every single swing.

[97]

Not Using Training Aids

Thousands of golf training aids have been invented throughout the years. Most of them ultimately don't pan out because they do not offer a reasonable solution to a golfer's specific problem. However, there are a few that have actually helped golfers improve.

Here is list of some of the better ones on the market that can help your game:

- **Swing Trainers:** Orange Whip, Tour Striker, and DST Compressor
- **Swing Analyzers:** Swingbyte, SkyPro, and Zepp
- **Putting Aids:** The Pill, TIBA Putt, and Birdie Ball

[98]

Playing the Wrong Tees

Some courses offer you a wide variety of tees to play from, and many golfers choose ones that are way too challenging for their games. If you are playing from tee boxes that are too difficult, then you will be forced into making aggressive decisions in order to feel like you are keeping up with the course.

It leads to more mistakes, and it's just not as fun.

The USGA came out with the Tee it Forward initiative a few years ago, and released the following chart as a guide for golfers:

Driver Distance	Recommended 18-Hole Yardages
PGA Tour	7,600-7,900
300	7,150-7,400
275	6,700-6,900
250	6,200-6,400
225	5,800 -6,000

These are reasonable recommendations, and if your course will allow you to play these yardages then you should consider following this guide. Playing from the back tees if you're not ready for the challenge will do more harm to your game than good.

[99]

Forgetting the Ball Needs to Remain in Play

One of the greatest tips for a tennis player is a simple one – keep the rally going. Most players try to go for the aggressive shot in an effort to win a point, and often it will lead to unforced errors. Had they just tried to keep the ball in play, it is likely their opponent might be the one making the mistake and losing the point.

This is no different in golf. Every decision you make on the course should accomplish one simple goal, which is to advance the ball towards your target with reasonable accuracy. It doesn't need to be perfect, or even above average.

You can hit a bunch of OK shots during your round and still shoot the score you are probably dreaming of.

It's the really bad shots that are the ones most likely holding you back, and they often occur when you are being too aggressive with your club selection or where you are aiming.

Before every shot try to keep this in mind, and remind yourself that your overall goal is just to keep the ball in play.

While it's easier than it sounds, this one simple goal can save you a ton of strokes.

Doing What Is Comfortable

Becoming a better golfer is mostly about changing your habits. If you keep doing the same thing over and over again, and you are still not improving, why keep doing it?

The easiest way to improve is to identify your weaknesses and work on them. The list doesn't have to be long. It could only be two or three things such as becoming a better chipper, or trying to make more putts from eight feet.

If you're comfortable hitting your driver, and that's all you work on in your practice sessions, then it's no surprise when you step up to that 80 yard wedge shot that your hands are shaking a bit more, and you can't commit to the shot.

The best part about working on your weaknesses is that you have nowhere to go but up! If you consistently waste strokes around the green because you mishit wedge shots, it might only take 5-6 practice sessions working on the proper technique to make something click in your head. That revelation alone could save tons of strokes.

Start thinking about the shots during your round that give you the most stress. Commit to figuring out how to play them effectively, and start devoting more of your practice sessions to them.

[101]

Never Visited Practical Golf

I hope you have enjoyed reading this book, but it wouldn't be complete without a plug for my website. Practical Golf was founded with the belief that while golf is a difficult game, it doesn't have to be complicated. I deeply believe that there are so many ways to lower your scores that aren't just about fixing your swing.

Come check out the site for articles, product reviews, and all kinds of talk on golf: www.practical-golf.com

My number one goal is to get golfers enjoying the game more, and hopefully improve their scores in the process. I hope to see you there!

Thank you for reading the book, and I hope you have a ton of ideas on how you can improve your golf game. Remember that you can't conquer all of these at once! Choose a few at a time, and go from there.

Made in the USA
San Bernardino, CA
10 June 2016